PROJECT SELF-DISCOVERY

Kendall Hunt
publishing company

Bethany Novotny, Ph.D. | Stacy Cummings Onks, Ph.D. | Michelle Hurley, Ed.D.

Cover image by Whitney Guyer Young

Kendall Hunt
publishing company

www.kendallhunt.com
Send all inquiries to:
4050 Westmark Drive
Dubuque, IA 52004-1840

Table of Contents

Preface

Abraham Maslow's hierarchy of needs posits that human beings have a driving instinct to self-actualize. In its most basic form, self-actualization is about finding joy in life, making meaning, and developing purpose. The payoff can be huge. It is a living, breathing concept that contracts and expands, morphs and refines, waxes and wanes but always remains. While there is no one path for every person, there are some personal landmarks that characterize a life well lived. Being able to confidently articulate values, effectively problem-solve, make meaning in your life, live healthily, find joy, and cultivate meaningful relationships are all hallmarks of a satisfying life. We can draw on our own experiences and the experiences of others to help us formulate an approach to life, but the value of intrinsic motivation to explore the richness of our world cannot be overestimated. In other words, you have the power to change your paradigm and it begins with a fervent desire to be your best self. Self-actualization is not necessarily a destination but the journey itself. Yet, the journey can be challenging without a clear path—a path that is not always linear. How do we know when we have gotten there? There is no handbook, no map, or no formula for completing this personal journey. Project Self-Discovery offers the tools to map a life of meaning that moves each student closer to their next best self.

The authors' intent when writing this book was to provide a platform for self-reflection and active exploration for each student who desired to carefully contemplate his or her past, present, and future. In the process of reading this book, you will be asked to "be brave, be honest, and be motivated" to examine your life trajectory. The book has been carefully chosen to guide you through the process and the activities designed to immerse you in the reflective excursion. Ultimately, as with any process, the value of the exercises will be directly affected by your genuine desire to learn and your active participation and effort with the materials.

*Portions of this book have been repeated from an earlier iteration of this text. These portions are noted by brackets throughout the present book.

Introduction

Abraham Maslow, the great American psychologist, once said "If the only tool you have is a hammer, you tend to see every problem as a nail" (Maslow, 1966). This quote underscores the power of limited thinking and the sometimes faulty reflections of our personal perception. It is entirely within reason to expect growth and change as your experiences expand and deepen. Yet, for many of us, we may find ourselves stagnant, stuck, and feeling as if we are in a state of inertia. As humans, we seemingly are predisposed to strive—to reach beyond what is currently in our grasp—and sometimes with this comes feelings of ineptitude, longing, jealousy, and frustration. Yet, that yearning to be something better, to challenge oneself and to progress toward the proverbial goal line is synonymous with growth.

For Maslow, growth was a central component of his theory of self-actualization. His idea that human needs range from the most basic (food, water, shelter) to the most noble (achieving one's full potential) resonates with our current culture. Maslow's hierarchy is depicted as a pyramid (See Figure 1) and theoretically an individual can move upward toward the highest level where self-actualization takes place.

According to the theory, lower level needs must first be met before subsequent levels can be addressed. Thus, the individual journey is hypothetically predictable, with one level building upon the other.

This book utilizes the theory posited by Maslow to illustrate the human instinct to self-actualize. In its most basic form, self-actualization is about finding joy in life, making meaning, and developing purpose. The payoff can be huge. Yet, the journey can be challenging without a clear path. One finds guidance where one can and the path is not always straight. Self-actualization is not necessarily a destination but the journey itself. It is a living, breathing concept that contracts and expands, morphs and refines, waxes and wanes but always remains. How do we know when we have gotten there?

For each person self-actualization may look different; however, you may be able to tell if you have reached this milestone by asking yourself the following question:

"Am I living my best life?" If your answer is a resounding "no", then it is likely that you are not fully actualized and may want to explore avenues that will help you improve those areas of life that are lacking.

While there is no one path for every person, there are some well-established tenets that characterize a life well-lived. Being able to confidently articulate values, effectively problem-solve, make meaning

©Pyty/shutterstock.com

FIGURE 1 Maslow's Hierarchy of Needs

in your life, live healthily, find joy, and cultivate meaningful relationships are all hallmarks of a satisfying life. Yet, there is no handbook, no map or no recipe for how to go about doing each of these things successfully. We can draw on our own experiences and the experiences of others to help us formulate an approach to life but the value of intrinsic motivation to explore the richness of our world cannot be overestimated. In other words, you have the power to change your paradigm and it begins with a fervent desire to be your best self.

How exactly is self-actualization operationalized? What does it look like? Maslow identified characteristics of self-actualizers (See Figure 2) and in later years focused on how self-actualization leads to transcendence or the experience of something extraordinary and beyond the normal scope of human existence (Kaufman, 2018).

16 Distinguishing Characteristics of Self-Actualizing people from the writings of Abraham Maslow

1. They are realistically oriented.
2. They accept themselves, other people, and the natural world for what they are.
3. They have a great deal of spontaneity.
4. They are problem-centered rather than self-centered.
5. They have an air of detachment and a need for privacy.
6. They are autonomous and independent.
7. Their appreciation of people and things is fresh rather than stereotyped.
8. Most of them have had profound mystical or spiritual experiences, although not necessarily religious in character.
9. They identify with mankind.
10. Their intimate relationships with a few specially loved people tend to be profound and deeply emotional rather than superficial.
11. Their values and attitudes are democratic.
12. They do not confuse means with ends.
13. Their sense of humor is philosophical rather than hostile.
14. They have a great fund of creativeness.
15. They resist conformity to the culture.
16. They transcend the environment rather than just coping with it.

FIGURE 2 Characteristics of Self-Actualizers

Republished with permission of John Wiley & Sons, from *Theories of Personality Study Guide*, Hall, C S, Hall, Calvin S, Lindzey, Gardner, © 1979; permission conveyed through Copyright Clearance Center, Inc.

As you review the list (Figure 2), you may be able to identify areas in which you are already living your best life, while others may be areas that you wish to improve. This is completely natural. While self-actualization can be viewed holistically, it can be valuable to begin your self-assessment by viewing the characteristics in isolation from one another. This provides context for planning and planning is often an integral part of growth.

This book may assist you as you travel toward self-actualization. Providing time to reflect on subjects varying from time management to service to wellness to financial competence, the text also contains exercises and activities to support your learning. Exploring and quantifying the components of your life journey can be both rewarding and daunting; however, it is worthwhile. If your desire is to "live your best life" then let's get started!

UNIT I

Define Your Identity

Image Description: Photo of the words "Who Am I?"

Who am I? What is my purpose in life? These are huge questions that everyone asks themselves at one point or another in life. We ask them, however, with some pressure to answer them, as though there is a definitive answer that we are supposed to uncover. Instead, could it be that we are constantly evolving and the answer that we are looking for is not static and unchanging, but rather always a work in progress. This may seem daunting, to search for answers to questions that may never be answered. Alternatively, we can see this as a challenge of self-growth and a lifelong commitment to discovering and rediscovering ourselves.

CHAPTER 1
Personal Identity Formation

Image Description: Photo of multiple gears with the words core values, trust, teamwork, ethics, etc. written on them.

This chapter has a very distinct purpose: to guide you through the first steps in a lifelong journey of self-identification and living your purpose. This process will assist you in developing the compass points to plot your life course as well as the skills to do so throughout your life.

In this first chapter, you will engage in some self-identity inventories and exercises that bring you to a better understanding of and appreciation for the most important and amazing person you will ever met....YOU!

In this chapter you will:

- Identify your core values and how you are living those values each day
- Explore your personality type
- Explore the concept of creating and maintaining life balance in all areas of your life
- Understand the different types of communications styles and skills along with those that you may want to increase your expertise in implementing
- Identify your motivations

Critical skill development: To develop a greater understanding for who you are, your life purpose, as well as launching the journey toward your best life. Even more importantly, this chapter wants to leave you with a strong skill set to continue this process throughout your life. The journey is yours and the course you plot is in your hands.

Values and Integrity

Question: Have you been asked to write down or enunciate in any way your core values?

The way you live and the choices you make reflect what is really important to you and provides you with insight into clarifying your personal values. In the best case scenario, these values drive all of our decisions, feelings, and actions, and represent the core of who we are. Our values reflect what is important to us and are really represented by where we invest our time and energy. They determine how we define success, what motivates us and how we express our needs and wants. They also serve as our guiding principles. Our values may be the most stable aspect or our emotional identity. Defining your personal values gives you the opportunity to evaluate the way in which you are living and to determine if you're truly living the way that reflects what is important to you as an individual. When you live according to your values, you feel confident and proud of the life you are living, as there is consistency between what you state as being important and the way you choose to live. Choosing to live without an awareness of your values often leads to self-defeating behaviors along with inconsistent and unsuccessful efforts toward achieving your goals. Your journey must begin with a strong and clear foundation—values identification. The following exercises will guide you along in that process.

VALUES IDENTIFICATION EXERCISE

Live Your Core Values

Core Values

Our core values are the true representation of our authentic selves.

Unfortunately, our authenticity is not always what we present to the world.

The bright beacon of core values may dim under the clouds of other people or circumstances. That is why it is important to know and stand firm on what your core values are. If you put a small value on your core values, we can assure you that the world will not raise your price!

It doesn't take years of soul searching and self-reflection to find your core values. This simple exercise can help you start living your best life according to your core values. How long will it take? About 10 minutes. Isn't it worth 10 minutes to refocus your life on your core values?

Grab a pen and piece of paper and let's go!

1. Determine Your Core Values

From the list below, choose and write down every core value that resonates with you. Do not overthink your selection. As you read through the list, simply write down the words that feel like a core value to you personally. If you think of a value you possess that is not on the list, write it down.

Abundance	Daring	Intuition	Resilience
Acceptance	Decisiveness	Joy	Resourcefulness
Accountability	Dedication	Kindness	Responsibility
Achievement	Dependability	Knowledge	Responsiveness
Adventure	Diversity	Leadership	Risk Taking
Advocacy	Empathy	Learning	Safety
Ambition	Encouragement	Love	Security
Appreciation	Enthusiasm	Loyalty	Self-Control
Attractiveness	Ethics	Making a Difference	Selflessness
Autonomy	Excellence	Mindfulness	Service
Balance	Expressiveness	Motivation	Simplicity
Being the Best	Fairness	Optimism	Spirituality
Benevolence	Family	Open-Mindedness	Stability
Boldness	Flexibility	Originality	Success
Brilliance	Friendships	Passion	Teamwork
Calmness	Freedom	Performance	Thankfulness
Caring	Fun	Personal Development	Thoughtfulness
Challenge	Generosity	Peace	Traditionalism
Charity	Grace	Perfection	Trustworthiness
Cheerfulness	Growth	Playfulness	Understanding
Cleverness	Happiness	Popularity	Uniqueness
Collaboration	Health	Power	Usefulness
Community	Honesty	Preparedness	Versatility
Commitment	Humility	Proactivity	Vision
Compassion	Humor	Proactive	Warmth
Consistency	Inclusiveness	Professionalism	Wealth
Contribution	Independence	Punctuality	Well-Being
Cooperation	Individuality	Quality	Wisdom
Creativity	Innovation	Recognition	Zeal
Credibility	Inspiration	Relationships	
Curiosity	Intelligence	Reliability	

2. Group All Similar Values Together from the List of Values You Just Created

Group them in a way that makes sense to you, personally. Create a maximum of five groupings. If you have more than five groupings, drop the least important grouping(s). See the example below.

Abundance	Acceptance	Appreciation	Balance	Cheerfulness
Growth	Compassion	Encouragement	Health	Fun
Wealth	Inclusiveness	Thankfulness	Personal Development	Happiness
Security	Intuition	Thoughtfulness	Spirituality	Humor
Freedom	Kindness	Mindfulness	Well-being	Inspiration
Independence	Love			Joy
Flexibility	Making a Difference			Optimism
Peace	Open-Mindedness			Playfulness
	Trustworthiness			
	Relationships			

3. Choose One Word within Each Group that Represents the Label for the Entire Group

Again, do not overthink your labels—there are no right or wrong answers. You are defining the answer that is right for you. See the example below—the label chosen for the grouping is **embolden**.

Abundance	Acceptance	Appreciation	Balance	Cheerfulness
Growth	Compassion	Encouragement	Health	Fun
Wealth	Inclusiveness	Thankfulness	Personal Development	**Happiness**
Security	Intuition	Thoughtfulness	Spirituality	Humor
Freedom	Kindness	**Mindfulness**	**Well-being**	Inspiration
Independence	Love			Joy
Flexibility	**Making a Difference**			Optimism
Peace	Open-Mindedness			Playfulness
	Trustworthiness			
	Relationships			

4. Add a Verb to Each Value Label

Add a verb to each value so you can see what it looks like as an actionable core value. For example:

> Live in freedom
> Seek opportunities for making a difference
> Act with mindfulness
> Promote well-being
> Multiply happiness

This will guide you in the actions you need to take to feel like you are truly living with a sense of purpose.

5. Finally, Post Your Core Values Where You See Them when Faced with Decisions

Where should you post them? Write your core values in order of priority in your planner, so they are available as an easy reference when you are faced with decisions. Put them on a sticky on the edge of your computer screen. Or make a background with them on it for your cell phone. For example:

1. Live in freedom
2. Act with mindfulness
3. Promote well-being
4. Multiply happiness
5. Seek opportunities for making a difference

Now Live Your Core Values!

If we can get to the place where we show up as our genuine selves, and let each other see who we really are, the awe-inspiring ripple effect will change the world.

Terrie M. Williams

The most important thing you can do for your personal success today is to know your core values and use them as your guide.

Knowing core values is important because when we need to choose or decide something, you can do so easily by simply determining if the choice lines up with your true core values. A life lined-up with personal values is a well-lived, purpose-filled life.

Congratulations on completing that exercise—it required a lot of introspection and some difficult decision making to get to YOUR *BIG 5* VALUES! The next step in defining your values is to construct your own value statements. Keep in mind that no two people will have the same value statements and the goal is for your value statements to most accurately reflect the way you want to live your life.

To take this value definition to the next step, follow the process below to give life to your values. Writing them down, seeing your values on paper makes them more concrete in your mind. This process gives them life and you a responsibility to them.

For each of your top 5 values, create the following statement:

"I choose/want to live my life in a way where _____ (state value) _____ by _____(state specific actions you will take to live out this value) _____.

Ex. I choose/want to live my life in a way where **"I nurture healthy relationships with my family, friends, and partner"** by **"being a good listener, traveling to see my family at least once a month and communicating about my life."**

LIFE JOURNEY PRO-TIP

You don't have to stop at 5 value statements. If you have other values that came out as a result of this exercise, challenge yourself to write out more key value statements in the above format OR modify to best fit your need.

It's time for the next leg of this values clarification journey—AM I LIVING MY VALUES? Take each value that you have identified through the following steps:

1) State your value clearly in construct form.
2) Do you honor this value in your daily living? If so, how?
3) In what ways do you dishonor your value in your daily living? (some text omitted)
4) How could you improve the ways that you honor this value in your living? How would you feel if you did honor your value more effectively?

Example:

- I choose to live my life in a way that supports getting a college degree so that I can work in my chosen career field.
- I read my chapters before each class. I go over my notes after each class and integrate it with my reading. I start studying for tests a week in advance. I start my class projects in plenty of time to do a good job.
- Sometimes. I do a good job of keeping up in some classes but procrastinate in others and do not have a clear plan after graduation.
- I will work more closely with my academic advisor and coach on time management to keep all classes rolling along well. Also, I will begin to work with career counselors to have a job search plan in place well before graduation. This would make me feel more in control of my post-graduation life.

Identifying Your Personality Type

Now that you have identified and articulated your values, it is time to embark on another path that may lead to even more insight—typing your personality. Personality typing is a framework for describing and explaining individual preferences, inclinations, and strengths. When we lack understanding of each other's personalities, personality clash can occur. Personality typing helps to demystify why we operate a certain way in our daily lives. The following example illustrates how individuals possess different constellations of characteristics that make them unique.

Image Description: Photo of a person with a T-shirt on that says "You are your own brand."

David is approaching his 23rd birthday and is planning a party to celebrate. He agonizes for several weeks over the guest list, checks in with his chosen venue multiple times and maintains carefully constructed lists that detail tasks that he is to complete before the party. He has acquainted himself with the rules and regulations associated with his event location and attended to every last detail of the catering arrangements.

Joyce's 23rd birthday is approaching. She also wants to host a party. She posts a general announcement on social media, inviting anyone who wishes, to meet at the park on the weekend and bring a covered dish with them. She spends little time planning and figures that things will naturally fall into place.

Both parties are a resounding success yet the approaches that David and Joyce chose were vastly different. David chose a more structured process, while Joyce chose a more laissez-faire method. What might this indicate about their respective personalities? For that matter, what is personality? Where does it come from and how do we accurately define it?

There are many definitions that have been posited. For example, Allport (1937) suggests that "personality is the dynamic organization within the individual of those psychophysical systems that determine his characteristics, behavior and thoughts" (p. 28). While Weinberg and Gould (1999) simplify somewhat and state that personality is "the characteristics or blend of characteristics that make a person unique" (p. 40). Whatever the definition, being able to accurately identify aspects of your personality and use that knowledge to better understand your motivations, values, behaviors, approaches, responses, and desires is a valuable life skill.

The study of personality is not new. In fact, scholars attempted to quantify and define personality as early as ancient Greece. Hippocrates, Plato, and Aristotle all proposed theories of personality in varying degrees of detail many of which centered upon the conjecture that personality traits were more philosophical in nature (McLeod, 2017). Later, personality was linked to physiological mechanisms, primarily via the case of Phineas Gage. Gage was a railroad worker, who was gravely injured by a tamping iron in 1848. During an accident, Gage's skull and brain were pierced clean through behind his left eye. He survived and was able to walk and talk; however, his personality was dramatically changed. According to reports of the time, Gage, who had been mild-mannered and jovial, became ill-tempered and morose, often crude (Cearhart, 2019). This instance was one of the first events that led researchers to believe that personality traits were anatomically seated.

There are two primary lenses for viewing personality theory—the idiographic view and the nomothetic view. The idiographic view suggests that each individual is unique and that some personality traits may only be observable in one person. Thus, comparisons between individuals are not possible (McLeod, 2017). The nomothetic view assumes that individuals can be compared because personality traits are static across all populations. Traits are viewed as if on a spectrum, with each individual falling along this spectrum in varying degrees.

One such theory that adopts the nomothetic approach is the personality theory developed by Carl Jung. Jung suggested that there were four psychological functions that individuals relied on in relation to personality formation—sensation, intuition, feeling, and thinking (Jung, 1971). He further stated that each individual tends to utilize one function dominantly (Jung, 1971).

During World War II, two researchers, Katherine Cook Briggs and Isabel Briggs Myers began to construct an instrument to measure individual personality traits based on the theory of Jung (Myers, 1980/1995). This assessment, now known as the Myers-Briggs Type Indicator (MBTI) is widely used to measure individual personality traits. An abbreviated version of this test is available online (Jung Typology Test). Let's find out what your personality type is!

Learning about your personality type and that of others helps you to:

- Understand our own preferences, inclinations, strengths and areas of needed improvement
- Be more aware of the roles that you accept at work, in relationships, etc.
- Discover ways to make changes that will increase your happiness and productivity.
- Leverage your strengths
- Deal more effectively with conflict and harmoniously work with others

FIGURE 1.1 Table of ways that learning about personality type may help you develop

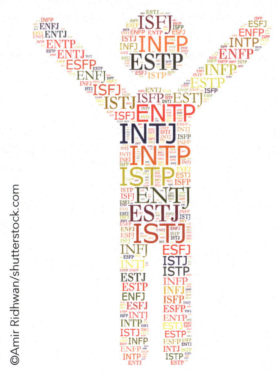

©Amir Ridhwan/shutterstock.com

Image Description: Illustrated person with the different types of personality descriptors written on their body

Exercise: Take Jung Typology Test

Scan the QR code to Take the Jung Typology Test

OR visit http://www.humanmetrics.com/cgi-win/jtypes2.asp

Now that you have completed the typology test, you should have received a four letter sequence (ESFJ, INFP, etc.) along with a number percentage for each letter. A better understanding of the letters and what they mean is necessary to accurately interpret your test. The Jung Typology Test, like the MBTI, is based on four different preference scales (Extraversion/Introversion, Sensing/Intuition, Thinking/Feeling, and Judging/Perceiving). According to theory, human behavior falls along a continuum on each of the four dimensions. The percentage that corresponds to the letter you received indicates how strong your preference is to think or act in that way. A low number indicates that you are more flexible on a particular dimension whereas a high number correlates with a strong tendency to gravitate toward that particular letter (more predictable).

Activity: Graph your percentages on the chart below.

The scale is as follows:

```
Extraversion -------------------------------- | --------------------------------Introversion
Sensing-------------------------------------- | --------------------------------Intuition
Thinking ------------------------------------ | --------------------------------Feeling
Judging-------------------------------------- | --------------------------------Perceiving
```

Although it is possible to have the same four letter sequence as someone else, your place along the continuum for each dimension can be unique. For example, both you and a friend may both be "E's" (extroverted) but your friend may be high on the spectrum (very much prefers extraversion) while you are lower on the spectrum nearer to the middle (somewhat prefers extraversion). Thus, you and your friend may react to situations differently even though you are both "E's". Keep in mind that there are numerous other factors that influence behavior, but this test can give you an idea of the way that individuals with certain typologies may react to their environment.

Let's examine each dimension and letter more closely. This can help you to better understand yourself and others.

There are four essential dimensions of personality type:

- Energy Style (Extroversion or Introversion)
- Cognitive Style (Sensing or Intuitive)
- Values Style (Thinking or Feeling)
- Self-Management Style (Judging or Perceiving)

Extraversion vs. Introversion (Energy Style)

This scale helps us to understand where we derive our energy from. The words themselves give you an idea, but once you understand this dimension, you will have a better idea of what energizes you and others.

Image Description: Illustrated people performing different activities with the words "Introvert or Extrovert—Open your secrets."

Energy style describes how we engage with others in our life, how we gain and expend our energy and whether we tend to process our thoughts out loud (verbally) or through introspection. Please note that this dimension should not be interpreted as describing individuals who like people and those who don't. It means that where people most likely find comfort and refreshment can differ. There is also the phenomenon of "crossover." This occurs when you purposely engage the less preferred side of your typology. For example, a normally extraverted person may take some time alone to read while a typically introverted individual may seek out group interaction. However, for most individuals there is the preferred manner of behavior that typically wins out.

Extroverts "External"

Extroverts tend to gain energy from external sources. Many extroverts:

- Focus outwardly
- Do first, think later
- Process thoughts out loud, with others. Enjoy the give and take of conversation
- Enjoy hands-on experiences and learning by doing
- Love to be involved in many different activities
- Prefers working with others
- May avoid solitude
- May enjoy organizing social outings—knows a great deal of people
- Speaks freely in meetings and enjoys the option to talk

Introverts "Internal"

Introverts tend to gain energy from looking inwardly. Many introverts:

- Focus inwardly
- Think before doing
- Process thoughts internally
- Tend to keep thoughts to themselves unless prompted to share
- Understand their environment by thinking it through
- Carefully pick and choose projects on which to work to ensure that they have adequate time to devote

- Find group events to be draining
- Can be easily overstimulated
- Needs ample time to spend alone to replenish energy stores
- Thrive in a quieter, calmer work environment

Sensing vs. Intuition (Cognitive Style)

This dimension focuses on how we prefer to take in information, what draws our attention, whether we focus on details or the larger picture and our preference for seeing data as it is or as it could be.

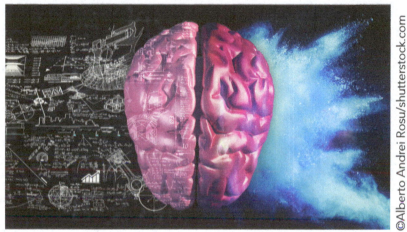

Image Description: Photo of a human brain with blue lights exploding from it

Sensing

Sensors rely heavily on information that they receive via their five senses (sight, touch, taste, hearing, and smell). They prefer to focus on:

- Sensory information
- Facts
- The present
- Concrete evidence

Sensors do not often interpret the data on their own, they more often simply describe observations in very literal terms with a focus on the here and now. In addition, sensors tend to:

- Avoid theoretical or abstract discussions
- Speak about the present and adhere to facts and evidence
- Be practical, literal, and methodical
- Enjoy routines and repetition
- Want concrete solutions to problems—avoid risky approaches

Intuition

Intuitives tend to see the possibilities that lie in the future. They see more than what is. They are adept at interpreting, analyzing, and making connections. They seek to make meaning out of data and prefer to focus on:

- Abstract concepts rather than details
- Future possibilities and potential options
- Connections and themes
- Their experience of something rather than just the facts

Intuitives are often excellent at "reading between the lines" and "going with their gut". They often:

- Bring a vibrant imagination and a visionary approach
- Are often seeking ways to improve a system and innovate
- Think in terms of "the forest" versus "the trees"
- Dislike mundane and repetitive routines
- Can easily become bored with average day-to-day activities

Thinking vs. Feeling (Values Style)

This dimension focuses on how we use data to make decisions. Our values style dictates not only our decision-making approach but also influences the conclusions that we draw from what we observe. Data is filtered through our personal values system based on our preference for logic and reason or empathy and personalization. Our values style also sways whether our sense of right and wrong is predicated on objective rightness and fairness or on individual circumstances.

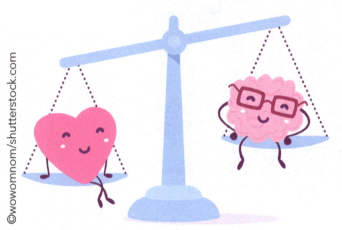

©wowomnom/shutterstock.com

Image Description: Illustration of scales with a heart on one scale and a brain on the other scale

Thinkers

Thinkers are often recognized for their objective and analytical approach to situations and decisions. That doesn't mean that thinkers lack empathy—it simply means that their preferred way of being involves thinking through matters carefully. Thinkers will want decisions to stand up to logic. When making a decision, thinkers will:

- Prioritize their thoughts over their feelings
- Seek verifiable data and evidence
- Tend to focus on more impersonal data
- Value objectivity and fairness

Thinkers also:

- May find it difficult to admit when they are wrong
- Enjoy debating
- Difficult to sway or influence once they have made up their mind
- Are more concerned with being fair than being liked
- Tend to speak in terms of "I think…"

Feelers

Feelers, on the opposite end of the spectrum, tend to make decisions based on their heart. Feelers are concerned less with objectivity and more with how their decisions will impact themselves and others. They prioritize relationships and emotional engagement. When making a decision, feelers tend to:

- Take individual concerns/circumstances more into account
- Wonder how the decision will affect others and relationships
- Take into account one's personal values and codes more so than logic and reason

Placing a significant emphasis on empathy and compassion, feelers often recognize that every situation is different and a one-size-fits-all approach may not work.
In addition, feelers often:

- Generally, demonstrate high EQ and are sensitive to others feelings and needs
- Eagerly identify with others
- Practice diplomacy and are careful with their words
- Tend to speak in terms of "I feel…"

Judging vs. Perceiving (Self-Management Style)

This dimension focuses on how you manage your time, your work, and your life events. Self-management refers to your manner of structuring your time and plans—whether spontaneous or methodical. It also involves your work patterns and the amount of information that you desire to have before making a decision.

Judgers

First, please note that being classified as a judger does not mean that you are judgmental! Judgers are ordered and prefer organization. They are the keepers of lists and tend to plan in advance. In addition, judgers prefer to:

- Schedule their time carefully
- Make a plan and then stick with it
- Prefer to achieve closure quickly
- Plan projects in advance and then structure their time to work on it in episodes

©Inked Pixels/shutterstock.com

Image Description: Person holding a crystal ball

Judgers tend to analyze a situation carefully and closely before giving their response but once a decision is made, they will forge ahead with gusto. Procrastination is not usually a problem for judgers as they prefer to get the job done quickly because they enjoy the feeling of accomplishment. Judgers also:

- Usually arrive on time or early
- Strive to set clear goals and objectives
- Relish having a schedule and want to stick with it
- Could be a little bossy or controlling
- Will be ready to make a decision, even without all the necessary information

Perceivers

On the opposite end of the spectrum, the perceivers thrive in environments where there is a great deal of freedom and flexibility. They enjoy innovation and change. They also prefer to collect as much information as they can before making a final decision. For perceivers, plans are made to be changed and many find this possibility exciting. Perceivers tend to:

- Take things as they come
- Collect information before making a decision
- Keep open-ended schedules
- Enjoy spontaneity

Remember that perceivers do not dislike structure per se, they simply have more difficulty imposing it on themselves. Perceivers do not like to be limited or stifled and can struggle when they are left with few options for achieving a goal or completing a task. Perceivers also:

- Will change a plan—even mid-task—when a better idea presents itself
- Tend to show up late
- Enjoy gathering as much information as possible before plotting a course of action
- Don't become too upset when plans or expectations change

It is important to note that no one type of personality is better than another. The purpose of identifying your personality type is to help you understand your own preferences and behaviors as well as those of others.

Now that you have read about and understand the four scales of this personality assessment, you are on the way to understanding your own personality type even more. Because there are four scales with a dichotomy on each, this means that there are a total of 16 different personality types. Here is a snapshot of the types:

The Sixteen Types

ISTJ *11.6%	ISFJ * 13.8%	INFJ *1.5%	INTJ *2.1%
ISTP *5.4%	ISFP *8.8%	INFP *4.4%	INTP *3.3%
ESTP *4.3%	ESFP *8.5%	ENFP *8.1%	ENTP *3.2%
ESTJ *8.7%	ESFJ *12.3%	ENFJ *2.5%	ENTJ *1.8%

* Frequency in population (Robinson, n.d.)

Put It Together

There are a myriad of resources that you can locate on the internet that will more fully explain your typology. Some helpful websites include:

- **https://www.16personalities.com/personality-types**
- **https://www.myersbriggs.org/my-mbti-personality-type/mbti-basics/the-16-mbti-types. htm?bhcp=1**
- **https://eu.themyersbriggs.com/en-IE/tools/MBTI/MBTI-personality-Types**

 Exercise: Personality Influences

Now, let's apply what you have learned to your everyday life. Read and answer the following questions, taking into consideration your personality type and how it influences your decisions and behaviors.

1. How do you approach a complicated task?

2. How might you respond to a friend whose mother has died?

3. How do you plan a trip?

4. What does your desk look like? Neat? Disorganized?

5. Where do you go to relax and what do you do there?

6. Describe your process for studying for an exam.

7. If you were serving on a criminal jury, what aspects of the case would be most important to you?

8. You are giving a lecture in front of 200 people. How would you prepare?

9. You are getting ready to purchase a new vehicle. How do plan to negotiate?

10. You must supervise another employee. How do you go about that?

Your personality style influences every aspect of your life experience—how you behave, what you think and how you feel. It certainly impacts the relationships that we cultivate with others. It can also influence how we approach tasks and measure success. Increasing your knowledge of personality types enables you to better understand yourself and others!

Temperament is another helpful term when considering one's approach to life. Most researchers agree that we are born with our temperament and that it remains stable throughout our lifetime. There are four different types of temperament. Take an internet time out to research the different types of temperament. Search term suggestions include: choleric, phlegmatic, sanguine, and melancholic.

Exercise ~ Developing a Corporation Based on Personality Influences

Divide into small groups—6–8 is ideal and then follow the instructions below.

You are members of a corporation that is looking to most efficiently organize itself. Based on your personality styles choose the members in your group to cover the following responsibilities. Justify your placement of individuals with information concerning their personality styles. You have to have someone in each of the roles. Some of the roles may be shared.

Identify the type of product or service your corporation is providing and then select individuals in your group for each of the following responsibilities based upon their personality traits.

Sales
Marketing
Accounting
Administration
Clerical Support
Engineering
Human Resources
Quality Control
Research and Development

Report

1. Identify who you placed in each role.
2. Identify the personality traits that justify your decision. List at least five traits to support each placement. Remember you can have more than one person in each role to complement each other's styles and each member of your group can have more than one role.
3. Once you have identified who is in the various roles discuss how you believe your corporation would work.

Exercise: Fire an Employee

For this exercise, you may do this as a group activity by dividing into groups of four to five or you may complete this as an individual activity. The purpose of this activity is to explore how different personality traits might affect our approach in a difficult situation—in this case—firing an employee that we supervise.

Give each individual/group the following scenario:

"Adam has been with your company for 5 years. He is 42-years-old, is married and has 3 children, ages 2–16. He has been under your supervision for the last 3 years. According to his performance evaluations, Adam did an excellent job for the first 4 years of his employment, however, during the last year his performance has dramatically decreased. He is unable to produce what is expected and his attitude has become negative. You have met with him several times to discuss his performance, but there have been no improvements. Today, you must fire Adam. Develop a plan for completing this difficult task, taking into account both how Adam will be effected as well as the company."

Discussion questions:
1. In what way did your own personality influence your approach?

    E vs I S vs N T vs F J vs P

Communication

As humans, we are in constant communication with one another. Even when you are alone in your room studying and your roommate is downstairs watching TV, you are communicating "I need to focus on studying at this moment, and watching TV with you does not allow me to get much studying done." However, your roommate may get the message, "I would rather sit in my room alone with my textbooks than watch TV with you." It is obvious that you cannot control anyone else or the way they receive your communication, whether it passes with words or not. What you *can* control is the *way* in which you communicate. We each have a personal responsibility to communicate in

Image Description: Illustration of two trees that are shaped like faces with birds flying between them

©Lightspring/shutterstock.com

a respectful, effective way, and although this doesn't always happen, below are some guidelines to follow that will help you when you are having difficulty communicating. These can be used in any relationship, no matter the depth or emotional involvement. Anytime you want to address something that is difficult or could be potentially hurtful, consider the following "commandments:"

THE 10 COMMANDMENTS OF CLEAN COMMUNICATION

Adapted from <u>Couple Skills: Making Your Relationship Work</u> by Matthew McKay, Patrick Fanning, and Kim Paleg (December 2006).

1. <u>Avoid judgemental words and loaded terms.</u>
   This relates to using terms that convey to your partner that he/she is flawed. Words that attack or undermine your partner's feelings of worth have no place in a caring relationship.
2. <u>Avoid global labels.</u>
   This relates to general condemnation of your partner. Such terms as stupid, sexist, crazy, selfish, etc. fall into this category. The outcome of using such words is a loss of trust and closeness.
3. <u>Avoid "you" messages of blame and accusation.</u>
   The essence of the you message is that, "I'm in pain and you did it to me." The message also reflects that, "you were bad and wrong for doing it to me." Use *I messages* that reflect ownership of your feelings instead.
4. <u>Avoid old history.</u>
   Good communication is succinct and focused. It sticks with the current issue and is specific. References to old history are often just building a case as to how bad your partner really is. It uses past transgressions to establish support for how bad your partner is and has no place in a good relationship.
5. <u>Avoid negative comparisons.</u>
   Negative comparisons only punish and put down your partner. A primary goal for a good relationship is to enhance your partner's self-esteem.
6. <u>Avoid threats.</u>
   The basic message of a threat is that you are or will be bad, and I will punish you if you are. Taking a position where you will inflict pain and/or suffering upon your partner is simply counterproductive.
7. <u>Describe your feelings rather than attack with them.</u>
   Describing your feelings provide clarification and promote enhanced understanding. Having a mutual understanding that feelings will be listened to and respected can contribute to a positive relationship. In

Image Description: Photo of a young child with goggles on talking through a tin can telephone

stating your feelings, it is helpful to keep your voice to a normal volume and inflection.

8. Keep your body language open and receptive.
Be aware that nonverbal communication is stronger than verbal. If you want your partner to listen or feel that you are listening it is important to maintain good eye contact, to use nonverbal cues to confirm that you are listening, to keep your body posture open, to model attentiveness, and to keep your face loose and relaxed.

9. Use whole messages.
Whole messages consist of observations, thoughts, feelings, and needs or wants. Observations are statements of facts that are neutral, without judgement, or interference. Thoughts are your beliefs, opinions, theories, and interpretations. Feelings are often the most important and simply describe the emotional state. Needs simply express what you want.

10. Use clear messages.
Clear messages separate observations, opinions, feelings, and needs. Communicating observations, opinions, feelings, and needs congruently bring consistency to your message and enhance your partner's understanding.

Here are some other helpful guidelines for positive communication:

- Express negative messages through words, but positive messages through both verbal and nonverbal channels.
- Focus upon each other with no distraction as working on something communicates the low value of the other's message.
- Allow time for each other to communicate and time to just be together. Providing such time demonstrates that you consider each other a priority. People also need time to be alone.
- Uncensored, open communication may be more than your relationship can handle. Be sensitive to other's touchy areas and approach them tactfully when you must. Timing can be critical.
- Avoid quarrelling over things that would have been better left unsaid. There are things about all of us that are difficult or even impossible to change. Acceptance may be far more productive than confrontation.
- People tend to weigh negative aspects of communication more heavily than the positive ones. Build positives if you really want the other person to hear you in a constructive way instead of just turning you off.
- Too many positive messages may reduce the level of social interaction.
- Nonverbal communication is generally more powerful than verbal.
- Explicit negative communications may be honest, but may be more destructive than helpful.
- Communication is a process of negotiation. Be attentive to bids and counterbids.

Implementing all these "commandments" and "guidelines" doesn't mean that changing the way you communicate is going to be as "easy as 1, 2, 3." In its most basic form, changing the way you communicate looks like this:

Five Steps to Communication Change

1. Listen.
2. Use measured self-expression.
3. Be selective at making requests.
4. Provide positive and corrective feedback.
5. Clarify communication so that the intended meaning is arrived at.

More than likely, you have communicated with a wide range of people in your lifetime. Some have been easy to talk to—you felt heard, understood, and respected—while others have been rude, selfish, and always thinking of what they will say next instead of focusing on what you are saying (or maybe you are guilty of those things yourself). Either way, we usually have no problem identifying those we can go to talk to, and those who are better with less serious conversations. To give you an idea, here are some characteristics of both good and bad listeners:

A Good Listener...

- Separates their emotions from other's words.
- Is fully committed to listening to others.
- Waits for the other to complete the message before expressing their own ideas.
- Uses analytic skills to supplement listening.

A Bad Listener...

- Rejects words from others as they are uninteresting, already known, too simple, or too complicated.
- Attends to the speaker's appearance and manner instead of to their spoken message.
- Stops attentively listening to the whole message and concentrates on a key word or phrase.
- Predicts what they will hear and fails to hear the real message.
- What kind of listener are you? Did reading these characteristics bring up anything in your personal life that is a good example of either?

It is clear at this point that no relationship can survive without healthy communication. You have probably heard friends or family members say "He just doesn't listen to anything I say!" or, "She never listens to my side of the story, always assuming she knows what I'm going to say!" Many couples decide to go to couples counseling with their main goal for therapy being, "We just need to learn to communicate." Communication also builds or breaks down friendships, family relationships, and work relationships. Adhering to clean communication is a way of respecting others, which is why when it is not practiced you tend to find discord in relationships.

A big part of clean and healthy communication is having the knowledge and awareness of its importance and how to implement it. Once you have that you can foster healthy relationships with minimal conflict. The sad reality is that conflict exists in every relationship in some form or another.

Life Balance and Wellness

Now that we have explored our personality type, let's turn our attention toward a healthy life balance and the concept of wellness. When you think about the words health or wellness, what comes to mind? Physical health is often the most common answer. Physical health can include a balanced diet, regular exercise, keeping up with preventative healthcare, and more. Physical health is definitely an important part of wellness; however, it is not the only one to consider. In fact, a

The part can never be well unless the whole is well

commonly accepted model of wellness includes six different areas that we should be attending to on a regular basis. This is called the Six Dimensions of Wellness Model and it is a holistic approach to the person, which includes emotional, intellectual, occupational, physical, social, and spiritual components of wellness. It is important to remember that you must make sure that each dimension is attended to in order to achieve holistic wellness. Just because you are healthy in one of the areas does not mean you are considered healthy from the Whole Person perspective. It takes work to be healthy in each of the areas and no one gets it right all the time, but being aware of the different areas of yourself that play a role in your wellness is a good first step toward evaluating and attaining a healthy, balanced life. We will take a more in-depth look at wellness in Chapter 5.

©Netfalls Remy Musser/shutterstock.com

Image Description: Photo of smooth rocks stacked on top of each other in a peaceful scene

The Six Dimensions of Wellness Model

Developed by Dr. Bill Hettler, co-founder of the National Wellness Institute (NWI), this interdependent model, commonly referred to as the Six Dimensions of Wellness, provides the categories from which NWI derives its resources and services.

A Description of Each Dimension

OCCUPATIONAL

The occupational dimension recognizes personal satisfaction and enrichment in one's life through work. At the center of occupational wellness is the premise that occupational development is related to one's attitude about one's work. Traveling a path toward your occupational wellness, you'll contribute your unique gifts, skills, and talents to work that is both personally meaningful and rewarding. You'll convey your values through your involvement in activities that are gratifying for you. The choice of profession, job satisfaction, career ambitions, and personal performance are all important components of your path's terrain.

Occupational wellness follows these tenets:
- It is better to choose a career which is consistent with our personal values, interests, and beliefs than to select one that is unrewarding to us.
- It is better to develop functional, transferable skills through structured involvement opportunities than to remain inactive and uninvolved.

PHYSICAL

The physical dimension recognizes the need for regular physical activity. Physical development encourages learning about diet and nutrition while discouraging the use of tobacco, drugs and excessive alcohol consumption. Optimal wellness is met through the combination of good exercise and eating habits. As you travel the wellness path, you'll strive to spend time building physical strength, flexibility and endurance while also taking safety precautions so you may travel your path successfully, including medical self-care and appropriate use of a medical system. The physical dimension of wellness entails personal responsibility and care for minor illnesses and also knowing when professional medical attention is needed. By traveling the wellness path, you'll be able to monitor your own vital signs and understand your body's warning signs. You'll understand and appreciate the relationship between sound nutrition and how your body performs. The physical benefits of looking good and feeling terrific most often lead to the psychological benefits of enhanced self-esteem, self-control, determination and a sense of direction.

Physical wellness follows these tenets:
- It is better to consume foods and beverages that enhance good health rather than those which impair it.
- It is better to be physically fit than out of shape.

SOCIAL

The social dimension encourages contributing to one's environment and community. It emphasizes the interdependence between others and nature. As you travel a wellness path, you'll become more aware of your importance in society as well as the impact you have on multiple environments. You'll take an active part in improving our world by encouraging healthier living and initiating better communication with those around you. You'll actively seek ways to preserve the beauty and balance of nature along the pathway as you discover the power to make willful choices to enhance personal relationships and important friendships, and build a better living space and community.

Social wellness follows these tenets:
- It is better to contribute to the common welfare of our community than to think only of ourselves.
- It is better to live in harmony with others and our environment than to live in conflict with them.

INTELLECTUAL

The intellectual dimension recognizes one's creative, stimulating mental activities. A well person expands his or her knowledge and skills while discovering the potential for sharing his or her gifts with others. Using intellectual and cultural activities in the classroom and beyond the classroom combined with the human resources and learning resources available within the university community and the larger community, a well person cherishes intellectual growth and stimulation. Traveling a wellness path, you'll explore issues related to problem solving, creativity, and learning. You'll spend more time pursuing personal interests and reading books, magazines, and newspapers, while keeping abreast of current issues and ideas. As you develop your intellectual curiosity, you'll actively strive to expand and challenge your mind with creative endeavors.

Intellectual wellness follows these tenets:
- It is better to stretch and challenge our minds with intellectual and creative pursuits than to become self-satisfied and unproductive.
- It is better to identify potential problems and choose appropriate courses of action based on available information than to wait, worry, and contend with major concerns later.

SPIRITUAL

The spiritual dimension recognizes our search for meaning and purpose in human existence. It includes the development of a deep appreciation for the depth and expanse of life and natural forces that exist in the universe. Your search will be characterized by a peaceful harmony between internal personal feelings and emotions and the rough and rugged stretches of your path. While traveling the path, you may experience many feelings of doubt, despair, fear, disappointment and dislocation, as well as feelings of pleasure, joy, happiness and discovery. These are all important experiences and components to your search and will be displayed in the value system you will adapt to bring meaning to your existence. You'll know you're becoming spiritually well when your actions become more consistent with your beliefs and values, resulting in a "world view."

Spiritual wellness follows these tenets:
- It is better to ponder the meaning of life for ourselves and to be tolerant of the beliefs of others than to close our minds and become intolerant.
- It is better to live each day in a way that is consistent with our values and beliefs than to do otherwise and feel untrue to ourselves.

EMOTIONAL

The emotional dimension recognizes awareness and acceptance of one's feelings. Emotional wellness includes the degree to which one feels positive and enthusiastic about one's self and life. It includes the capacity to manage one's feelings and related behaviors including the realistic assessment of one's limitations, development of autonomy, and ability to cope effectively with stress. The well person maintains satisfying relationships with others. Awareness of, and accepting a wide range of feelings in yourself and others is essential to wellness. On the wellness path, you'll be able to express feelings freely and manage feelings effectively. You'll be able to arrive at personal choices and decisions based upon the synthesis of feelings, thoughts, philosophies, and behavior. You'll live and work independently while realizing the importance of seeking and appreciating the support and assistance of others. You'll be able to form interdependent relationships with others based upon a

foundation of mutual commitment, trust, and respect. You'll take on challenges, take risks, and recognize conflict as being potentially healthy. Managing your life in personally rewarding ways, and taking responsibility for your actions, will help you see life as an exciting, hopeful adventure.

Emotional wellness follows these tenets:
- It is better to be aware of and accept our feelings than to deny them.
- It is better to be optimistic in our approach to life than pessimistic.

Applying the Six Dimensions of Wellness Model

By applying the model, a person becomes aware of the interconnectedness of each dimension and how they contribute to healthy living. This holistic model explains:

- how a person contributes to his or her environment and community, and how to build better living spaces and social networks;
- the enrichment of life through work, and its interconnectedness to living and playing;
- the development of belief systems, values, and creating a world-view;
- the benefits of regular physical activity, healthy eating habits, strength and vitality, as well as personal responsibility, self-care and when to seek medical attention;
- self-esteem, self-control, and determination as a sense of direction;
- creative and stimulating mental activities, and sharing your gifts with others.

Applying a wellness approach can be useful in nearly every human endeavor. As a pathway to optimal living, wellness is being applied to related fields, such as health promotion and holistic health, and has seen a growth in "helping professions" including counseling and medical arts and practices. The National Wellness Institute devised three questions that can help persons and organizations assess the degree to which wellness is incorporated into a particular approach or program:
- Does this help people achieve their full potential?
- Does this recognize and address the whole person (multi-dimensional approach)?
- Does this affirm and mobilize people's positive qualities and strengths?

Evaluating your Life Balance

Consider each of six dimensions of wellness and determine how important, if at all, each area is to you.

1. Rank each area of wellness in order of how much they influence your happiness (1–6, 1 being the most influential).

   _1_ Emotional
   _6_ Intellectual
   _4_ Occupational
   _2_ Physical
   _3_ Social
   _5_ Spiritual

2. For each area of wellness, consider how happy you are with this area of your life, what you would want to change in that area, and how you might implement this change.

Emotional Wellness Description: Being able to make comfortable to change and handle aspects of life

Changes I would like to make: I wouldn't make any

Emotional goal(s):
→ Social awareness
→ Self Care

Intellectual Wellness Description: Recognizing all abilities and grow our knowledge

Changes I would like to make: I wouldn't make changes

Intellectual goal(s):
→ Be better at making Problems better
→ Be better at taking Instruction

Occupational Wellness Description: Gives People the ability to Explore options

Changes I would like to make: wouldn't make any

Occupational goal(s): • Increase my Goals
• Become a Leader for another Breed

Physical Wellness Description: Maintaining a healthy Living

Changes I would like to make: wouldn't Change anything

Physical goal(s): Eat healthy
Gain weight

Social Wellness Description: To help People in need

Changes I would like to make: help everyone be less Selective

Social goal(s): Change lives
make People happy

Spiritual Wellness Description: abiding by values and beliefs

Changes I would like to make: nothing I would change

Spiritual goal(s): Get closer with the man above
Get out here

End of Chapter Self-Reflection

With each chapter, you are growing and developing more self-awareness. Climbing the steps toward becoming your best self. At the end of each chapter, you will be presented with a series of stair steps to capture your progress. Wherever you are is ok! Respond to each open-ended prompt on the staircase and save your answers for the culminating planning session at the end of the course.

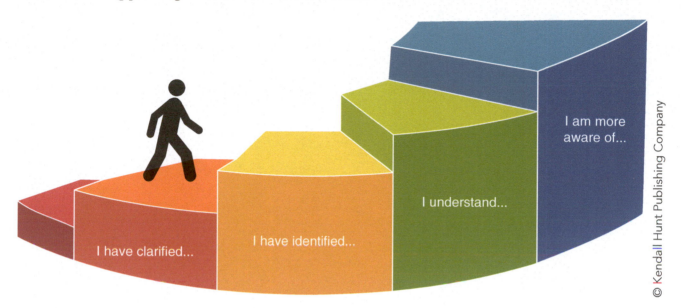

I have clarified...

I have identified...

I understand...

I am more aware of...

© Kendall Hunt Publishing Company

References

Allport, G. W. (1937). *Personality: A psychological interpretation.* New York, NY: H. Holt.

Cearhart, S. (2019). Phineas Gage. *Encyclopedia Britannica.* Retrieved from https://www.britannica.com/biography/Phineas-Gage

Jung, C. G. (1971). "Psychological types." In *Collected works of C. G. Jung* (Vol. 6). Princeton, NJ: Princeton University Press.

Maslow, A. (1966). *The psychology of science.* Chicago, IL: Chicago-Gateway.

McLeod, S. (2017). Theories of personalities. Retrieved from https://www.simplypsychology.org/personality-theories.html

Myers, I. B., with Myers, P. B. (1995). *Gifts differing: Understanding personality type.* Mountain View, CA: Davies-Black. (Originally published 1980)

Robinson, M. T. (n.d.). How rare is your personality type? Retrieved from https://www.careerplanner.com/MB2/TypeInPopulation.cfm

Weinberg, R. S., & Gould, D. (1999). Personality and sport. *Foundations of Sport and Exercise Psychology,* 25–46.

CHAPTER 2
Cognitive Processes

Image Description: A tree in the shape of a brain being watered by a watering can

The purpose of this chapter is to better understand your thought processes and how you make decisions.

In this chapter you will:

- Learn the skills associated with critical thinking
- Develop an awareness of growth mindset
- Explore your process for making decisions and solving problems
- Increase your awareness of the importance of curiosity and lifelong learning

Critical skill development: To increase awareness of how your thoughts influence your behavior and to establish a framework for decision making and problem solving.

Curiosity and Lifelong Learning

Your engagement in this course is indicative of your innate curiosity to learn and grow. The process of self-growth and learning is, and should be, a lifelong process. The wisest people know they never know everything. This is a big, wonderful world full of mysteries with fascinating people, places, and things. Being curious about these fascinations will energize your life and motivate you to engage in an ever widening circle of knowing and being.

Image Description: Photo of a person's hands opening a door to see a blue sky with the word "Learning"

There are times when you might be engaged in a course or activity that does not seem interesting or of use to you. Learning to find the purpose in every activity will be an attitude enhancer and help even the mundane and trivial activities take on new meaning. In other words, it is your attitude toward the activity or course that makes the difference!

Image Description: Illustration of an open book in the midst of a peaceful scene

One student shared,

I had to take two US History courses for part of my general education requirements in college. I had already had US History like every year of my school life through 12th grade it seems like. So I was not really pumped at all about having to do this and only paid enough attention in the class to get the grade I wanted. Honestly though, I did have to study because I didn't exactly retain information from before. I am not gonna lie, I was pretty ambivalent about it. When I graduated, I moved 2400 miles away from family and friends. I was anxious to get a job and get established to feel more secure so far away from the life I knew. I had a master's degree and some part time job experience, nothing much on the resume really. I was in an interview and saw all the other candidates in the waiting room. I didn't really think I had a shot at the job working with adults with disabilities because that job experience was not at all on my resume, but I was desperate for a job. Part of the interview was lunch with the program director. During the lunch conversation, she asked questions about my interest in the job, resume, etc. Then there was just casual conversation for her to get to know me. She started talking about herself a bit and indicated a passion for history and her favorite era. By some miracle, I could recall some of the information I remembered from my US history class and could talk to her about this interest. Totally unrelated to this job, but making conversation. Three days later, I get a call and I had gotten the job! I couldn't believe it. The director said that I was selected because I was more well-rounded in my knowledge base than the other candidates—from our casual conversation about history!! So that is when I realized, even information that may not be my jam could be of use to me. I think that is the real moment I opened my eyes to everything around me and became a curious lifelong learner.

This is the "aha moment" for a student that shifted their mindset to one of engaged wonder in the experiences in front of them rather than the apathetic learning that was not engaged. In today's age of instant and constant information, so much information comes at you so quickly and in such an entertaining presentation that it is hard to process even a fraction of it on a daily basis.

> The two most important days in your life are the day you are born and the day you find out why.
>
> Mark Twain

©Yury Zap/shutterstock.com

Image Description: The quote "The two most important days of your life are the day you are born and the day you find out why." Mark Twain

Attitude

There is a saying that you have probably heard more than once in your life, "you can achieve anything if you put your mind to it!" Have you ever wondered how your mindset impacts the achievement of goals? Or how different people excel at different rates, even when they have similar talents and circumstances? Two constructs have emerged as important contributions toward understanding how people achieve and perform to the best of their abilities: grit, which can be defined as "perseverance and passion for long-term goals" and entails "working strenuously toward challenges, maintaining effort and interest over years despite failure, adversity, and plateaus in progress" (Duckworth, Peterson, Matthews, & Kelly, 2007, p. 1087), and mindset, which refers to one's belief about one's personal characteristics as being either fixed or malleable (Dweck, 2006).

©Cristina Conti/shutterstock.com

Image Description: Illustration of a person with a telescope sitting on a large stack of books

Mindset

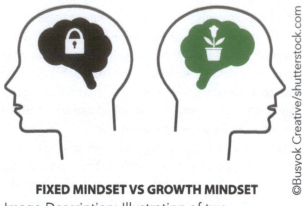

©Busyok Creative/shutterstock.com

FIXED MINDSET VS GROWTH MINDSET

Image Description: Illustration of two
people—one with a lock on their brain and
the other with a flower and the words "Fixed
versus growth mindset"

Dweck (2006) described mindset very simplistically as "the view you adopt for yourself" (p. 6); however, mindset is anything but simple. According to Dweck (2000), there are two distinct mindsets: fixed (entity

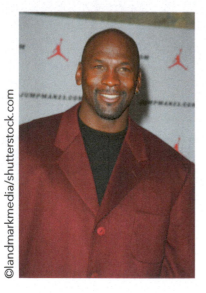

©landmarkmedia/shutterstock.com

theory) and growth (incremental theory). A fixed mindset is characterized by a belief that one has only a certain amount of intelligence, static personality, and unchanging character, which leads individuals to repeatedly attempt to prove themselves or to avoid potential failures. Individuals with a fixed mindset thrive when success is certain. These individuals often choose the safest path to achievement to maintain a positive image, either for themselves or for others (or both).

A growth mindset, in contrast, is characterized by the belief that qualities, including intelligence, can be changed and cultivated through awareness, efforts, and hard work (Dweck, 2000). Individuals with a growth mindset view challenges as opportunities for growth and development, despite the potential for failure (Dweck, 2006). Individuals with a growth mindset do not linger over failure but, in fact, have proven to be growth-oriented, focusing on learning from previous experiences, applying the knowledge that was gained, and improving performance (Elliott & Dweck, 1988). Dweck (2006) used a quote from Michael Jordan to exemplify the growth mindset:

"I've missed more than 9000 shots in my career. I've lost almost 300 games. Twenty-six times, I've been trusted to take the game winning shot and missed. I've failed over and over and over again in my life. And that is why I succeed" (p. 100).

In addition to two distinct mindsets, Dweck (2000) identifies two response patterns (mastery-oriented and helpless) to adversity or failure and two types of achievement goals (learning and performance). A **mastery-oriented** response is characterized by increased focus, persistence despite adversity, and more vigorous effort to match increased difficulty. A **helpless response pattern**, conversely, is characterized by blaming intelligence for an inability to complete demanding tasks, deterioration of effort as difficulty increases, and loss of perspective on accomplished success (Dweck, 2000).

Performance goals involve maintaining positive judgements and preserving one's positive image (Dweck, 2000). Therefore, individuals will set goals or take on tasks that they know they can accomplish with ease to avoid any negative judgements about their attributes (Hong, Chiu, Dweck, Lin, & Wan, 1999). **Learning goals**, in contrast, are specifically intended to be challenging to provoke growth and to increase skill and mastery, despite the possibility of failure (Dweck, 2000). Individuals with a growth mindset typically set learning goals and tend to have mastery-oriented responses to adversity or failure, and individuals with a fixed mindset typically set performance goals and tend to have helpless responses (Dweck, 2000). Implicit theories, or "mindsets," have been studied considerably in the areas of social psychology and education. Mindset has been demonstrated to have significant effects on psychological functioning, especially in stressful situations (Schroder, Dawood, Yalch, Donnellan, & Moser, 2015).

According to Karwowski (2014), holding a fixed versus a growth mindset regarding one's abilities influences well-being, behavior, and goal attainment. The beliefs that one holds regarding his or her abilities influences how much and for how long effort is exerted toward a particular goal (Federici & Skaalvik, 2012). A fixed mindset often leads individuals to lose interest or enjoyment in a task if it becomes too challenging or threatens to be a task they cannot complete, whereas, for growth-minded individuals, the harder the challenge, the more invested they become (Dweck, 2006). In other words, a fixed mindset is about perfection, and a growth mindset is about progress.

Grit

Grit is defined as passion and perseverance for long-term goals (Duckworth et al., 2007) and has two related but distinct factors: effort and interest (Von Culin, Tsukayama, & Duckworth, 2014). Kelly, Matthews, and Bartone (2014) defined grit as an unswerving, sustained, and passionate pursuit of a given interest or goal. Grit has been advanced as one of the most important factors toward success in life (Tough, 2013). Grit can be thought of as a character strength that reflects one's capacity for resilience, self-discipline, and persistence over time despite challenges, failures, and plateaus in progress (Duckworth et al., 2007). Grit differs from resiliency with its focus on longevity and persistence over time rather than on short-term intensity (Duckworth et al., 2007). Grit, in essence, is the determination to work diligently and persist through inevitable adversity to accomplish long-term goals without losing interest or willpower, with little regard for the possibility of failure.

Image Description: Photo of a cup of coffee, a notebook, pen, and a cactus with the words "New mindset—new results"

Image Description: Illustration of three puzzle pieces with the words persistence, grit, passion

Image Description: Photo of a cup of coffee, piece of paper and a pen with the words "Success starts in the mind."

Duckworth et al. (2007) found that individual differences in grit accounted for variance in success outcomes over and beyond IQ and the Big Five personality factors. Individuals who are equally talented or have a similar skillset may vary in grit and, therefore, vary in their amount of success in a given area. Gritty individuals tend to pursue long-term goals without changing course, concentrate more effort in one particular area, and complete tasks in their entirety (Duckworth et al., 2007). Gritty individuals persist even when it may be easier to give up or switch directions (Lucas, Gratch, Cheng, & Marsella, 2015). Grit has been shown to protect against divorce, job loss (including in education and business professions), leaving the military, and dropping out of school (Eskreis-Winkler, Shulman, Beal, & Duckworth, 2014). An individual's effort and persistence in overcoming difficulties may lead to the promotion of a more positive mindset and greater self-efficacy (Federici & Skaalvik, 2012).

Image Description: Picture of the words, "The devil whispered in my ear, 'You're not strong enough to withstand the storm.' Today I whispered in the devil's ear, 'I am the storm.'"

Importantly, neither grit nor growth mindset are permanent characteristics. Dweck and Leggett (1988) found that a fixed mindset can lead to maladaptive helpless responses, avoidance, lower success and engagement in social domains, and decreased persistence. In contrast, having a growth mindset can lead to greater internal motivation, higher self-esteem, and exhibit a strong desire to set and achieve goals (Dweck & Leggett, 1988). Mindset (fixed or growth) is the worldview we adopt for ourselves regarding our intelligence and abilities and it is something we have control over (Dweck, 2006). Like mindset, grit also is not a fixed trait. It has been suggested that having a growth mindset could develop grit (Hochanadel & Finamore, 2015).

Image Description: Illustration with the words attitude, behavior, action, performance, results surrounding the word mindset.

Image Description: Photo of a person writing a goals list

Activity

List some accomplishments that you have that demanded a lot of time, energy, and dedication:

Short Grit Scale

Directions for taking the Grit Scale: Please respond to the following 8 items. Be honest – there are no right or wrong answers!

1. New ideas and projects sometimes distract me from previous ones.*
   - ❏ Very much like me
   - ❏ Mostly like me
   - ❏ Somewhat like me
   - ❏ Not much like me
   - ❏ Not like me at all

2. Setbacks don't discourage me.
   - ❏ Very much like me
   - ❏ Mostly like me
   - ❏ Somewhat like me
   - ❏ Not much like me
   - ❏ Not like me at all

3. I have been obsessed with a certain idea or project for a short time but later lost interest.*
   - ❏ Very much like me
   - ❏ Mostly like me
   - ❏ Somewhat like me
   - ❏ Not much like me
   - ❏ Not like me at all

4. I am a hard worker.
   - ❏ Very much like me
   - ❏ Mostly like me
   - ❏ Somewhat like me
   - ❏ Not much like me
   - ❏ Not like me at all

5. I often set a goal but later choose to pursue a different one.*
   - ❏ Very much like me
   - ❏ Mostly like me
   - ❏ Somewhat like me
   - ❏ Not much like me
   - ❏ Not like me at all

6. I have difficulty maintaining my focus on projects that take more than a few months to complete.*
   - ❏ Very much like me
   - ❏ Mostly like me
   - ❏ Somewhat like me
   - ❏ Not much like me
   - ❏ Not like me at all

7. I finish whatever I begin.
   - ❑ Very much like me
   - ❑ Mostly like me
   - ❑ Somewhat like me
   - ❑ Not much like me
   - ❑ Not like me at all

8. I am diligent.
   - ❑ Very much like me
   - ❑ Mostly like me
   - ❑ Somewhat like me
   - ❑ Not much like me
   - ❑ Not like me at all

<u>Scoring</u>:

1. For questions 2, 4, 7 and 8 assign the following points:
   5 = Very much like me
   4 = Mostly like me
   3 = Somewhat like me
   2 = Not much like me
   1 = Not like me at all

2. For questions 1, 3, 5 and 6 assign the following points:
   1 = Very much like me
   2 = Mostly like me
   3 = Somewhat like me
   4 = Not much like me
   5 = Not like me at all

Add up all the points and divide by 8. The maximum score on this scale is 5 (extremely gritty), and the lowest score on this scale is 1 (not at all gritty).

Grit Scale citation

Duckworth, A.L, & Quinn, P.D. (2009). Development and validation of the Short Grit Scale (Grit-S). *Journal of Personality Assessment, 91*, 166-174.
http://www.sas.upenn.edu/~duckwort/images/Duckworth%20and%20Quinn.pdf

Duckworth, A.L., Peterson, C., Matthews, M.D., & Kelly, D.R. (2007). Grit: Perseverance and passion for long-term goals. *Journal of Personality and Social Psychology, 9*, 1087-1101.
http://www.sas.upenn.edu/~duckwort/images/Grit%20JPSP.pdf

Development and Validation of the Short Grit Scale (Grit-S), Angela Lee Duckworth, Patrick D. Quin, *Journal of Personality Assessment*, 2/17/2009, Taylor & Francis, reprinted by permission of the publisher (Taylor & Francis Ltd, http://www.tandfonline.com).

Activity: Goal Setting

List some long-term goals that you would like to accomplish

1.

    ❑   Tasks that will help me accomplish this long-term goal:

    ❑   Strategies to keep myself motivated:

2.

    ❑   Tasks that will help me accomplish this long-term goal:

    ❑   Strategies to keep myself motivated:

3.

    ❑   Tasks that will help me accomplish this long-term goal:

    ❑   Strategies to keep myself motivated:

4.

    ❑   Tasks that will help me accomplish this long-term goal:

    ❑   Strategies to keep myself motivated:

Now, under each long-term goal you've identified, brainstorm some short-term or medium-term tasks that will help you accomplish the long-term goal. For example, you may want to earn a graduate degree (long-term) but one of your first steps would be to identify a program and apply (short/medium-term). Next, identify some strategies for how you will keep yourself motivated, even when life throws you obstacles. Here are a few suggestions: keep the end goal in mind, journal about your progress, plan a reward for yourself when you reach a short-term goal, find a lesson in the setbacks.

Finally, think about learning versus performance goals. Go back through your list and try to identity each of your goals as learning or achievement by placing the appropriate letter next to your goal: L = Learning or P = Performance

Critical Thinking

"The experts use the metaphorical phrase critical spirit in a positive sense. By it they mean 'a probing inquisitiveness, a keenness of mind, a zealous dedication to reason, and a hunger or eagerness for reliable information.'"
Facione, P.A. (2015, p. 2)

Attitude, curiosity, grit, and mindset are all vitally important in a well-lived life. Let's introduce another important skill to our toolbox—critical thinking. How many times have you been in a classroom and heard your professor say, "I want you to use your critical thinking skills"? Perhaps you have encountered syllabi or grading rubrics that identify critical thinking as integral. Critical thinking has become a buzz word in the academy and is often used as an umbrella term for a host of skills that may seem abstract and elusive. Yet, the demand for the ability to think critically remains constant for both professors and for prospective employers. If critical thinking is so important, then a clear definition is needed. Furthermore, we need to identify and operationalize the components of critical thinking so that skills can be developed. Let's get started!

Image Description: Illustration of a cyclical process with the words "Critical thinking."

Researchers and educators have proposed many different definitions of critical thinking (web search critical thinking and see!). But perhaps more important than a definition is the recognition that critical thinking involves a series of steps that evolve in a logical order. Learning to work through these steps successfully can lead you to a creative and inventive way of thinking. Why is this important? It is important because we are faced with many decisions every day, some that may be inconsequential—others that can change the course of our lives. Critically thinking through a decision can increase the chance that your decision-making process is sound and more likely to lead to the outcome that you desire. Additionally, the ability to think critically enhances your aptitude to develop creative solutions to problems.

Image Description: Illustration of a magnifying lens with the words "Critical thinking."

It may be helpful to start with what is *not* critical thinking. Memorization, although necessary and helpful at times, is most certainly not a part of critical thinking. In his writings on critical thinking, Facione states "considered as a form of thoughtful judgment or reflective decision-making, in a very real sense critical thinking is pervasive. There is hardly a time or a place where it would not seem to be of potential value" (Facione, 2015, p. 3). So critical thinking is a skill that must be practiced but has a place almost anywhere and everywhere in your life. Let's see what components or steps are involved in thinking critically according to Facione.

CRITICALTHINKING

Image Description: The words "Critical thinking" in bright colors

CORE CRITICAL THINKING SKILLS		
SKILL	**DEFINITION**	**SUB-SKILL**
Interpretation	"To comprehend and express the meaning or significance of a wide variety of experiences, situations, data, events, judgements, conventions, beliefs, rules, procedures, or criteria"	■ Categorize ■ Decode significance ■ Clarify meaning
Analysis	"To identify the intended and actual inferential relationships among statements, questions, concepts, descriptions, or other forms of representation intended to express belief, judgement, experiences, reasons, information, or opinions"	■ Examine ideas ■ Identify arguments ■ Identify reasons and claims
Inference	"To identify and secure elements needed to draw reasonable conclusions; to form conjectures and hypotheses; to consider relevant information and to reduce the consequences flowing from data, statements, principles, evidence, judgements, beliefs, opinions, concepts, descriptions, questions, or other forms of representation"	■ Query evidence ■ Conjecture alternatives ■ Draw logically valid or justified conclusions
Evaluation	"To assess the credibility of statements or other representations that are accounts or descriptions of a person's perception, experience, situation, judgment, belief, or opinion; and to assess the logical strength of the actual or intended inferential relationships among statements, descriptions, questions, or other forms of representation"	■ Assess credibility of claims ■ Assess quality of arguments that were made with inductive or deductive reasoning
Explanation	"To state and to justify that reasoning in terms of the evidential, conceptual, methodological, criteriological, and contextual considerations upon which one's results were based; and to present one's reasoning in the form of cogent arguments"	■ State results ■ Identify procedures ■ Present arguments
Self-Regulation	"Self-consciously to monitor one's cognitive activities, the elements used in those activities, and the results deduced, particularly by applying skills in analysis, and evaluation to one's own inferential judgements with a view toward questioning, confirming, validating, or correcting either one's reasoning or one's results"	■ Self-monitor ■ Self-correct

From *Critical Thinking: What It Is and Why It Counts* by Peter A. Facione. Copyright © by Insight Assessment. Reprinted by permission.

Let's simplify the concept by offering an example of critical thinking. You and a friend are debating the value of the death penalty in the United States. Your friend is arguing that the death penalty is an effective deterrent while you are arguing the opposite—you disagree that the death penalty is an appropriate means of punishment or deterrence. As you listen to your friend, you begin to recognize patterns (categorize) and clarify the meaning of their words (clarify meaning). Using all of your senses, you decipher which ideas or beliefs are significant to your friend (decode significance). You use this opportunity to ask questions that help you to discern their thoughts and feelings and address any terms that may be ambiguous (clarify meaning). During this INTERPRETATION stage, your main goal is to take in large amounts of data and make meaning of it by categorizing, recognizing themes, and clarifying terms that may be unclear. It is best to remain calm and focus on genuinely understanding the person's position, refrain from ar-

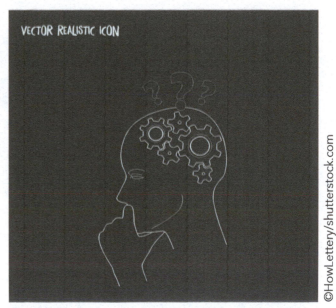

VECTOR REALISTIC ICON

©HowLettery/shutterstock.com

Image Description: Illustration of a person with gears in their headspace

guing your point, just listen and ask clarifying questions. It is of importance to note that the process of critical thinking is a two-way street. You are also INTERPRETING your own thoughts by asking internal questions of yourself and clarifying your own feelings. **The attention to your own thoughts and feelings will continue throughout this entire process.**

After you and your friend have made your initial statements, you may realize that they have a very clear stance on the subject and now you can begin to further ANALYZE what your friend said. At this stage you more fully examine their ideas by continuing to ask clarifying questions. Your friend might have said that they believe in the death penalty for all murderers. You might further clarify this for example by asking if that also applies to women who are victims of domestic violence who retaliate. At this point, you can begin to develop clearer ideas of your friend's arguments ("So do you mean..."), better identify the reasons that they think or feel that way and decipher any claims that they are making to support their argument (identify reasons and claims). Your friend may have cited a research statistic that posits that the death penalty is utilized successfully 95% of the time—95% of executed inmates are guilty of the crime that they were incarcerated for. Furthermore, your friend may argue that in the interest of fairness and justice, that one person's life must be paid for by the perpetrator's demise. This is still not the time to start arguing your point. Rather it is time to organize your thoughts and ensure that you fully understand what your friend is saying as well as what you are saying (self-analysis).

At the next stage, your questioning may become more pointed. This is the time to ask your friend for additional evidence that supports their position (query evidence). This is not the time to argue the validity of the evidence that is offered it is simply a time to gather as much additional evidence as you can to help inform your opinion and to clarify that of your friend's. It is also time to present your own evidence supporting your opinion. And then one of the most important parts of the process takes place—thinking of alternative ways to process the issue. This is important because it marks a possible turning point in the conversation. Could your mind be changed? Could your friends mind be changed if you both viewed the issue from a different perspective (conjecture alternatives). Spending some time looking at alternative viewpoints is time well spent. In the end, it may not change your opinion or that of your friend, but it is a valuable exercise in dissecting the complexity of an issue. Finally, you begin to draw conclusions about your own thoughts as well as those of your friend's. The conclusions should be logical based on the evidence that has been presented (draw logical conclusions)

©Kirasolly/shutterstock.com

Image Description: Picture of a complex brain

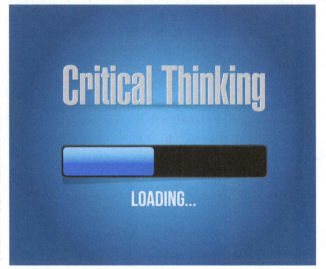

©alexmillos/shutterstock.com

Image Description: Illustration of a computer loading icon with the words "Critical thinking."

and refine the arguments further by succinctly stating suppositions. During this INFERENCE stage, you may find that abstract arguments become more concrete and concise.

In the EVALUATION stage, the rubber really hits the road! During this stage, you continue to flex your critical thinking muscles by carefully appraising the quality of the evidence that has been presented in order to support your arguments. This can be tricky because people often have strongly ingrained ideas of what type of evidence is worthwhile and sound. For example, one person might value the statistics of a peer-reviewed research publication, while another may value the word of their father or mother. Both of these sources can be credible; however you have to examine the credibility within the context of the issue you are discussing (assess credibility of claims). In this case, you might return to the earlier statistic that your friend presented—95% of those who are executed are guilty. You may posit a question asking where your friend found that statistic—was it a credible, non-biased source? Was it recent? Did it apply to the U.S., etc.? Next you will assess the quality of the arguments that both you and your friend are making. First, is the argument a product of sound deductive or inductive thinking (a logical progression of thought)? Next, does the argument stand up to further questioning. For example, at this point you may ask your friend to explain what happens to the 5% of people who are executed who are innocent and ascertain how that caveat informs their opinion.

During the EXPLANATION stage, things start to firm up. This is the point where you can more clearly state your position (state results); however, it is always helpful to establish the procedures that you completed to reach that position (identify procedures). In other words, you explain the logical route that you took to arrive at your conclusion. For example, you may say that based upon recent statistics, you have concluded that the death penalty is not effective. You may also cite more subjective sources such as your own value system and beliefs but if you do, be prepared to be challenged. Objective evidence is often stronger than subjective evidence. An example of subjective evidence might be one's religious views. So, in stating your conclusion, you might add that your specific religious affiliation prohibits the death of any person. This is still relevant but might lack the authority of more objective evidence. Nevertheless, often our stances are governed by both objective and subjective information. Once you have clearly exchanged the reasons why you believe the way that you do, you can be better prepared to present your argument more effectively. During this stage the dialogue goes back and forth as arguments are presented, accepted, and/or rejected. This is also a point where minds can be changed when presented with new evidence.

Self-regulation takes place throughout the entire critical thinking process. When one self-regulates, they practice self-reflection and correction. This occurs at every stage—as you are formulating, refining,

Image Description: Illustration of a brain lifting a bar bell of books

and presenting your arguments. This is an exercise in discipline and involves the ability to question one's own conjectures and clarify whether or not logic is being utilized. It also may have an emotional component as well. When we are debating topics, we can tend to become emotionally charged and invested in our own argument. This in and of itself is not necessarily a negative thing but it can be if your emotions override your ability to think logically and coherently. Self-regulation enables one to monitor their motivations and accurately appraise the evidence that they are relying on to make their case.

Do you know what the difference is between objective evidence and subjective evidence? Take an internet time out to see what you can find!

Activity: Critical Thinking Mindset Self-Rating Form

Answer Yes or No to each question. **Can I name any specific instances over the past 2 days when I:**

1. Was courageous enough to ask tough questions about my longest held and most cherished beliefs?
2. Backed away from questions that might undercut some of my longest held and most cherished beliefs?
3. Showed tolerance to the beliefs, ideas, or opinions of someone with whom I disagreed?
4. Tried to find information to build up my side of the argument but not the other?
5. Tried to think ahead and anticipate the consequences of various options?
6. Laughed at what other people said or made fun of their opinions, beliefs, or point of view?
7. Made a serious effort to be analytical about the foreseeable outcomes of my decisions?
8. Manipulated information to suit my own purposes?
9. Encouraged peers to not dismiss out of hand the opinions and ideas that other people offered?
10. Acted with disregard for the possible adverse consequences of my choices?
11. Organized for myself a thoughtfully systematic approach to a question or issue?
12. Jumped in and tried to solve a problem without first thinking about how to approach it?
13. Approached a challenging problem with confidence that I could think it through?
14. Instead of working through a question for myself, took the easy way out and asked someone else for the answer?
15. Read a report, newspaper, or book chapter or watched the world news or a documentary just to learn something new?
16. Put zero effort into learning something new, until I saw the immediate value in doing so?
17. Showed how strong I was by being willing to honestly reconsider the decision?
18. Showed how strong I was by refusing to change my mind?
19. Attended to variations in circumstances, contexts, and situations in coming to a decision?
20. Refused to reconsider my position on an issue in light of differences in contexts, situations, or circumstances?

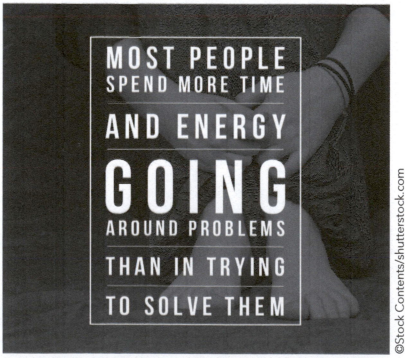

Image Description: Picture with the words, "Most people spend more time and energy going around problems than in trying to solve them.

Instructions for Scoring

"If you have described yourself honestly, this self-rating form can offer a rough estimate of what you think your overall disposition toward critical thinking has been in the past 2 days. Give yourself 5 points for every "Yes" on odd numbered items and for every "No" on even numbered items. If your total is 70 or above, you are rating your disposition toward critical thinking over the past 2 days as generally positive. Scores of 50 or lower indicate a self-rating that is averse or hostile toward critical thinking over the past 2 days. Scores between 50 and 70 show that you would rate yourself as displaying an ambivalent or mixed overall disposition toward critical thinking over the past 2 days. Interpret results on this tool cautiously. At best this tool offers only a rough approximation with regard to a brief moment in time" (Facione, 2015, p. 14).

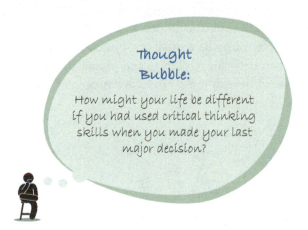

Thought Bubble:

How might your life be different if you had used critical thinking skills when you made your last major decision?

Being adept at critical thinking may produce better outcomes in your life. By using the tools discussed here, you are more likely to make informed decisions, competent assertions, and compelling arguments. These skills are not only important for your future career but important as you navigate relationships and other areas of your life. Don't forget, your critical thinking muscles must be exercised frequently in order to be as effective as possible!

Further Reading

Dobelli, R. (2013). *The art of thinking clearly*. New York, NY: HarperCollins.
Ryan, J. E. (2017). *Wait, what?* New York, NY: HarperCollins.
Weston, A. (2009). *A rulebook for arguments*. Indianapolis, IN: Hackett.

Internet Search Keywords:

Critical thinking, argumentative debate, logical thinking, rationale

Problem Solving

Now that you have your critical thinking cap on, let's explore its connection to problem-solving. Before you initiate the internal eye roll when you see the words "PROBLEM SOLVING", remove those two words and replace them with "CREATIVE THINKING". That is really all problem solving is—creatively thinking your way through a situation. Think back to moments when you were really motivated to get something you wanted but had an obstacle to getting it. Begging your family for a puppy, trying to get your first car, figuring out how to afford that vacation you wanted, anything. To get that "thing", you had to be pretty creative to work it out. SO, you know you have that skill—it is time to learn how to deploy that skill successfully and in multiple situations.

This section is designed to develop problem-solving skills via creative thinking that will be useful to you throughout your life. It is an important skill to cultivate, as it is oftentimes the problems you encounter that stall forward momentum. The problem may be a small one but can quickly become bigger than it really is for lack of having an action-oriented strategy for resolution and procrastinating.

The goal is to guide you toward developing a process or processes that will be successful for you in any situation for problem resolution.

Here we go!

©iQoncept/shutterstock.com

Image Description: Illustration of a puzzle with the words "Whatever it takes."

Step ONE: GETTING READY TO TAKE ON THIS PROBLEM/CHALLENGE! Cultivating a growth minded attitude of positivity, creativity, resourcefulness and confidence.

POSTIVITY: YOU ARE IN CONTROL OF THE PROBLEM; IT DOES NOT CONTROL YOU! This step prepares you to acknowledge your strengths and resources to address the problem or situation at hand. This is about your headspace. You have just learned about critical thinking as well as growth and fixed mindset. Take a moment to consider how you can apply these concepts to your problem-solving plan.

Guiding questions:

- What do I know about a growth mindset?
- What concepts from critical thinking will support me here?

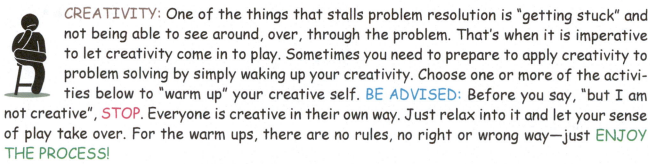 CREATIVITY: One of the things that stalls problem resolution is "getting stuck" and not being able to see around, over, through the problem. That's when it is imperative to let creativity come in to play. Sometimes you need to prepare to apply creativity to problem solving by simply waking up your creativity. Choose one or more of the activities below to "warm up" your creative self. BE ADVISED: Before you say, "but I am not creative", STOP. Everyone is creative in their own way. Just relax into it and let your sense of play take over. For the warm ups, there are no rules, no right or wrong way—just ENJOY THE PROCESS!

It is time to wake up BOTH sides of your brain. The left side of your brain specializes in logic, practical or pragmatic thought and things like mathematics. The right side of your brain excels in the creative, imaginative, artistic and intuitive side of things. For effective brainstorming you need to have both sides of your brain firing well!

Activity: Creativity Warm-Up

Directions. Grab a piece of paper and pen, pencil, crayon—your choice. Choose one of the figures below. Take your pencil and try to make each little figure into something else. You can do whatever you want with these. You can make them funny or beautiful. You can add words. You can use more than one at a time—whatever you want. There is no right or wrong here. Take your time and enjoy the process of waking your creative self. When you feel AWAKE, move on to the next step!

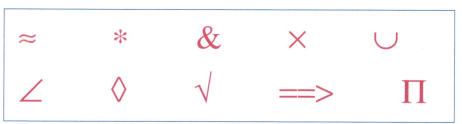

Activity: Resource, resiliency, and protective factors list

- People in my corner:

- My skills that can be used in solving this problem:

■ Past experiences and learning that I can draw from in this situation—successes or misses in solving problems:

■ Financial resources:

■ Community resources:

■ Anything else I can think of:

NOW YOU ARE READY TO SOLVE A PROBLEM!

ONE WAY TO ATTACK THE PROBLEM—FORWARD OR LINEAR PROBLEM SOLVING

You are in the right mindset; all you need is a strategy for solving a problem or overcoming an obstacle. Here is a simple strategy or process that should work for you. For this exercise, you may choose a problem or obstacle that is important to you in using this process, but one is suggested for purposes of this exercise.

Step 1. IDENTIFY THE PROBLEM

Direction. It is important in this step to be as specific as possible and put in some details after the problem statement. Free writing or drawing can be helpful at this stage. Do not focus on writing super fancy statements or impressive sentences. Just simple, clear statements with detail.

Problem statement (example): I have difficulty addressing problems and tend to let them just hang around for a while. I really procrastinate and let them build up which sort of makes them bigger than they were to begin with. I get really stressed out and don't really know where to start to make this problem go away. So when this happens, I usually just do something else so I am not thinking about the problem.

Step 2. IDENTIFY THE COMPONENTS OF THE PROBLEM

Direction: List the components or aspects of the problem that is in front of you. Break the larger problem down into smaller parts. Once you have the list of the smaller components, highlight or circle the components that you think is key to the root of the problem. You could also start with the component that you could readily solve to move yourself forward. The goal at this point is to break down the larger problem and address the smaller aspects of this problem to propel you toward resolution.

Pro Tip: Any step forward is a reason to celebrate, so choose aspects of the problem that you can readily fix and then move on to the next.

Components of my problem (example):

1. I don't know where to start. I can't really settle down in my thoughts. I may panic a little when I think about the problem.

2. I follow the same plan (or non-plan) that I have used in the past

3. Procrastination is HUGE for me when I am dealing with problems

4. The stress from not taking care of the problem actually becomes bigger than the problem. The stress of it almost makes it impossible for me to react to the situation. So I guess I need some better stress management skills too.

5. I do not have a clear path or plan to resolve problems.

6. Sometimes I am not sure of the outcome I am working toward when I am trying to handle a problem. What I mean is, what is the healthiest solution for me?

Step 3. GET YOUR BRAIN OUT OF THE BOX

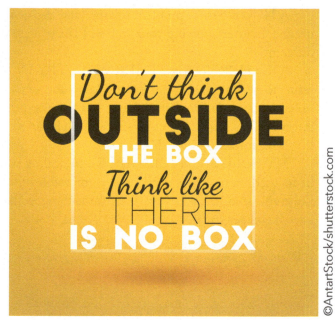

Image Description: Words "Don't think outside the box. Think like there is no box."

Directions: List some possible solutions to the problem. Let your brain go on super-drive and identify any, all, large, small, sensible, ridiculous, outrageous, possible, impossible solutions to this problem. List them all here. DO NOT hold back—there are no limitations on this one. By allowing yourself to free think and imagine all options, nothing is left out. This is the point where you just get all down and then choose the best of the options you have in front of you or devise better options as you process this.

Pro Tip: Keep a note pad and pen handy during this phase so when an idea comes to you, you can jot it down. A healthy pro-tip at this phase is exercise. Sometimes, getting out for a walk, hike, run, yoga class, meditation, golf…whatever, will help you with ideas and possibilities.

Possibilities:

■ Draw out my problem solving strategy—I am more visual so seeing it might help

■ Research some problem solving strategies on the internet. Pick your top 3 and try one of them.

■ Put the different parts of the problem on note cards/post-it notes and put them on your wall. Then you can move them around as you see potential solutions.

■ Schedule time in your day to sit and work through the possibilities. Make it a priority to attack this problem and resolve it so you can move on to better things.

■ Include some motivational readings, inspiring music, whatever that will keep you in the headspace you need to be in to resolve this.

■ Work with a life coach, supportive friend, anyone in your "village" to talk through ideas and to help keep you accountable to resolving this issue.

Step 4. ACTION PLAN

Now that you have worked through the first three steps, you have the information you need to come up with ACTION to solve your problem. A n action plan should be specific and include time-frames for accomplishment. The same concept in developing your action plan are the same steps that are used for goal setting. Skip forward to the Chapter on SMART goals and use that outline for your problem solving action plan.

A HUGE part of problem solving (and also goal setting) is to evaluate your plan and make adjustments as needed. If, after applying your Action Plan, you are not pleased with the outcome, you need to try something different.

AND HERE'S ANOTHER WAY—TRY IN REVERSE! Sometimes you know what you want the end result to be, but you do not exactly know the steps you need to get there. This problem solving technique is called Backwards Problem Solving and there is quite a bit of information on this technique to review on the internet. This is actually quite simple. You begin at the END! In other words, answer the following question for the example used for this exercise:

MY SOLUTION (EXAMPLE): In dealing with problems I have; I will attend to them right away and be focused on resolving until I feel comfortable with the outcome. No more procrastinating and stressing out. From this solution, you work backwards through the steps. Some problems are solved best this way, so give it a try if you get stuck.

Want to learn more? Here are some suggested readings to build on the work you have completed in this section:

How to Think Like Leonardo da Vinici: Seven Steps to Everyday Genius by Michael Gelb

Inspiration Sandwich: Stories to Inspire Our Creative Freedom by Sark

Wreck this Journal by Keri Smith

Questions for Reflection:

- What is my current problem solving strategy?
- Does it work?
- Am I proactive with follow-up and follow through?
- Do I procrastinate at any of the steps?

Internet Search Words:

Creative thinking
Problem solving
Backwards problem solving
Procrastination
Healthy stress management

End of Chapter Self-Reflection

Now it's time to reflect on what you learned in this chapter on cognitive processes. Respond to each open-ended prompt on the staircase and save your answers for the culminating planning session at the end of the course.

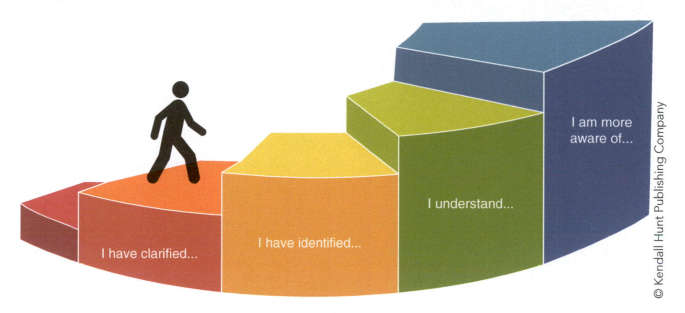

References

Duckworth, A. L., Peterson, C., Matthews, M. D., & Kelly, D. R. (2007). Grit: Perseverance and passion for long-term goals. *Journal of Personality and Social Psychology, 92*(6), 1087–1101. doi:10.1037/0022-3514.92.6.1087

Dweck, C. S. (2000). *Self-theories: Their role in motivation, personality, and development.* New York, NY: Psychology Press.

Dweck, C. S. (2006). *Mindset: The new psychology of success.* New York, NY: Ballantine Books.

Dweck, C. S., & Leggett, E. L. (1988). A social-cognitive approach to motivation and personality. *Psychological Review, 95*(2), 256–273. doi:10.1037/0033-295X.95.2.256

Elliott, E. S., & Dweck, C. S. (1988). Goals: An approach to motivation and achievement. *Journal of Personality and Social Psychology, 54*(1), 5–12. doi:10.1037/0022-3514.54.1.5

Eskreis-Winkler, L., Shulman, E. P., Beal, S. A., & Duckworth, A. L. (2014). The grit effect: Predicting retention in the military, the workplace, school and marriage. *Frontiers in Psychology, 5*(36), 1–12. doi:10.3389/fpsyg.2014.00036

Facione, P. A. (2015). Critical thinking: What is it and why it counts? *Inquiry, 28*(1), 1–29.

Federici, R. A., & Skaalvik, E. M. (2012). Principal self-efficacy: Relations with burnout, job satisfaction and motivation to quit. *Social Psychology of Education, 15*(3), 295–320. doi:10.1007/s11218-012-9183-5

Hochanadel, A., & Finamore, D. (2015). Fixed and growth mindset in education and how grit helps students persist in the face of adversity. *Journal of International Education Research, 11*(1), 47–50. Retrieved from http://cluteinstitute.com/ojs/index.php/JIER/article/viewFile/9099/9098

Hong, Y., Chiu, C., Dweck, C. S., Lin, D., & Wan, W. (1999). Implicit theories, attributions, and coping: A meaning system approach. *Journal of Personality and Social Psychology, 77*(3), 588–599.

Karwowski, M. (2014). Creative mindsets: Measurement, correlates, consequences. *Psychology of Aesthetics, Creativity, and the Arts, 8*(1), 62–70. doi:10.1037/a0034898

Kelly, D. R., Matthews, M. D., & Bartone, P. T. (2014). Grit and hardiness as predictors of performance among West Point cadets. *Military Psychology, 26*(4), 327–342. doi:http://psycnet.apa.org/doi/10.1037/mil0000050

Lucas, G. M., Gratch, J., Cheng, L., & Marsella, S. (2015). When the going gets tough: Grit predicts costly perseverance. *Journal of Research in Personality, 59*, 15–22.

Schroder, H. S., Dawood, S., Yalch, M. M., Donnellan, M. B., & Moser, J. S. (2015). The role of implicit theories in mental health symptoms, emotion regulation, and hypothetical treatment choices in college students. *Cognitive Therapy and Research, 39*(2), 120–139. doi:10.1007/s10608-014-9652-6

Tough, P. (2013). *How children succeed: Grit, curiosity, and the hidden power of character.* Boston, MA: Mariner Books.

Von Culin, K. R., Tsukayama, E., & Duckworth, A. L. (2014). Unpacking grit: Motivational correlates of perseverance and passion for long-term goals. *The Journal of Positive Psychology, 9*(4), 1–7. doi:10.1080/17439760.2014.898320

UNIT II

Why Am I Here? Exploring Purpose and Awareness

Image Description: Words "Find your purpose" with a red heart.

In this unit we explore finding your life purpose(s) and assess needs of transcendence. Higher-order tasks such as making meaning of your life, cultivating gratitude, serving others and being culturally responsive and engaged will be tackled. Answering the question "why am I here?" is central to this unit.

CHAPTER 3
Self-Transcendence

Image Description: Person with a glowing heart sitting in a peaceful scene

©Benjavisa Ruangvaree Art/shutterstock.com

In this chapter, self-transcendence is explored, which occurs when we put aside our own needs to serve something greater than ourselves. Our need to be of value and to be affirmed is central to our well-being. How better to gain this affirmation, than to be in the service of others and purposefully practicing gratitude.

In this chapter, you will:

- Increase your capacity for finding meaning and joy in your life
- Learn how to approach life with gratitude
- Explore opportunities to serve others
- Practice living with intent and formulating goals

Critical skill development: To approach your life in a way that is inclusive of others and cognizant of their needs. In addition, these practices could engender a sense of fulfillment and purpose in your life that may have been elusive before!

Image Description: Sign with the words "Do something today that your future self will thank you for."

Making Meaning and Finding Joy

We are all unique with special gifts to share. The challenge is to find out what those gifts are and how we are going to best share them. This sharing of our gifts brings us into a life that is full of meaning and purpose. At different junctions in the road, your life purpose may become unclear or you may challenge what you have previously identified as your meaning for being. This chapter is intended to offer an introspective process to serve you at any stage of your life when you want to evaluate your "WHY" for being.

For many people, making meaning in their life is a daily practice, and for some, it is a carrot dangling just out of reach. The goal in this moment is to define your life goals. To do that, some concept definition needs to happen. To get your thinking going, answer the following questions:

1. Making meaning in my life looks like:

2. How do I describe or define joy?

3. What habits do I have that inhibit joy? Cultivate joy?

4. What can I let go of that might allow me to have more joy? What do I need that could bring me more joy?

5. Who or what gets in the way of joy in my life?

There is an inner feeling of wellness when you are living a life that is congruent with your values, your idea of living up to your potential and with clear goals that guide you along the way. Making meaning and finding joy in your life seems like a no-brainer life goal. Yet, this goal can easily get lost in the shuffle of daily living. You wake up on Monday morning and before you know it, it is Friday after your workweek ends and nothing other than the "have to's" of your life have occurred and even some of that has not happened. The pace of your daily life can be an obstacle to meaningful living. So, let's think about pace! Please take some time to answer the following questions:

1. What does your daily life look like?

2. How is your energy best spent?

3. Is this where you would like your best energy to be spent?

4. Do you need to make changes? If so, what is one of the first changes you would make?

5. Are you running your life or is your life running you?

6. What or who is determining the pace of your life?

Now that you have taken some time to answer these questions, where is your time going? Where is your time going? Are these activities taking you closer to your goals, contribute to your whole wellness, and in alignment with your values? (it might be helpful to log your activities for a couple of days—see activity log in Chapter 6).

There are many current and past writings that challenge us to look at the pace of our lives and why we have adopted a culture where being *busy* is equated with a full life. Other writers and philosophers offer up the same challenge. At this point, you are asked to take a pause in the reading and complete the following exercise for reflection.

NOTE: This is not "homework" or a traditional "assignment", this is purely, 100% for you. The following explorations are suggestions to get you going and may lead to other thought trails you would like to pursue—DO IT! The beauty in this exercise is that you cannot get it wrong, it is research for you and by you with the intent of opening your eyes to other ways of thinking about your life and the meaning you are making. SO, YOU WILL GET OUT OF IT WHAT YOU INVEST INTO IT! Also, how often in a course are you encouraged to surf the web, so enjoy!

Do an internet search on the following, see what pops up and where it leads you:

Total wellness
Crazy busy
Living with intent
Purposeful living
Pace of life
The Positive Project

Here is a short list of authors/books that you might want to check out. Choose at least three to read an overview of the book provided online and see if any of them speak to what you are feeling right now.

Eckhart Tolle *in Praise of Slowness*
Richard Louv *the Nature Principle*
Edward Hallowell *Crazy Busy*
Sherry Turkle *Reclaiming Conversation in the Digital Age*
Daniel Golemen *Focus*
Brene Brown *Daring Greatly*
Randy Pausch *the Last Lecture*
Desmond Tutu *the Book of Forgiving*
Dalai Lama, Desmond Tutu, et al. *The Book of Joy: Lasting Happiness in a Changing World*
Maya Angelou *Rainbow in the Cloud: The Wisdom and Spirit of Maya Angelou*

Some journaling often helps. You will be prompted to complete some guided journaling later in the chapter. Some examples of guided journaling are:

Keri Smith *Wreck This Journal*
Gretchen Rubin *Happiness Project*

Living with Intent

Finite Heart Beats

A woman in her 50s was reflecting with lifelong friends on a broken relationship and all the time she had devoted to attempting to make the relationship work over many years. During those years, she felt the effort at the relationship was one-sided and she truly never got what she wanted from her partner. After talking this through at length, she went away to ponder it all. When her friends gathered again, she said she would like to share her reflection. She had come to the conclusion that at her current age, she realized that she had a finite number of heartbeats left and she was not going to waste any one of them on anyone or anything that did not bring her joy or contribute to the good she could do in the world. She concluded with a challenge to the friend group to live in the same way AND to share with their children, so that this lesson was learned earlier rather than later in life. *No wasted heartbeats!*

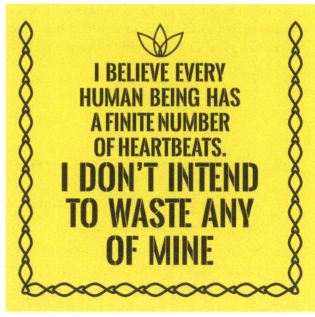

Image Description: The words "I believe every human being has a finite number of heartbeats. I don't intend to waste any of mine" on a yellow background

Why worry about finite heartbeats? We have plenty of them and plenty of time to figure out what we want to do with these heartbeats. In a conversation with a student, one advisor reported that their graduate student, Andrew, was upset. Andrew was 27 years-old and had been continuously in school for his whole life. As he was preparing to graduate, he realized he did not have a clear life path and he was nearing 30 years old. He was distressed and felt rudderless. This is similar to some others described in the book, The Defining Decade" Meg Jay. In this book, Dr. Jay focuses on making the most of your twenties so that the 30s, 40s, 50s and beyond have great meaning. The messages are relevant and generalizable at any life-stage. When you have a moment, take a look at this book.

There are other individuals who have realized that their heartbeats are finite and are doing all they can to make them most of them. This is a moment to take a page from the playbook of a little girl named Elena Desserich. A little girl who at only 6 years of age made an enormous impact on her world. In Notes Left Behind, her parents share her amazing story. There are inspiring individuals at all ages, races, and cultures that prompted this thought about using your heartbeats meaningfully and may motivate you to consider how you are spending your heart beats!

Internet Surfing Break: Take an internet surfing moment to Google the names of Elena Desserich, Iqbal Masih, Jack Andraka, Boyan Slat, Malala Yousafzai…and many others. Look for people who inspire you to make the most of your heartbeats.

Fortunately for us, the list of this amazing young people making the most of their heart beats is a long one. From their example, the challenge is to set your own course. Make your own mark, be it big or small. These words are easy to type and encourage you to do an air fist pump and say "Yeah, I am gonna jump up right now and go dig a well so someone can have clean drinking water, or go protest a cause, or….." Then the doubts of what should become your

Image Description: The words "Live less out of habit and more out of intent."

mark begin to surface and lead to indecision or inaction. It is easier to turn back to your electronic device and surf the web or social media or anything that distracts you from taking that first step toward making meaning. You need a plan! That plan can mirror the problem-solving exercise that we discussed in Chapter 2.

Activity Time Out

Your turn! How can you live with intent? Here's an idea of how it could work:

Step 1.   Doodle, write, draw, record your ideas for your life and what is important to you.

Step 2.   Choose the top 3 that you are interested in improving, exploring, and initiating right now.

Step 3.   Identify one activity for each that could be a first step.

Step 4.   DO IT! If you cannot make a decision, pick any service project or self-improvement activity and try it! The idea is to do something!

Having trouble getting started?

Internet Surfing Break Search the web for these terms to get ideas and suggestions.

Getting unstuck
Creative thinking
Problem solving
Procrastination

During your time working with the information in this unit, the goal is to begin to define your purpose in life, to make meaning of that purpose by living with intention and in joy. This is not a one and done event, rather a process that is lifelong and changes as you grow. Ideas that you will be exploring and defining are what you believe your purpose to be or what you want it to be, how you can live with intent, and your definition of joy. The heart of this process is reflecting on questions to promote introspection.

While engaging with this unit, there are some questions to reflect upon as you read through this material. You may have other questions, ideas, or thoughts that you would like to add as a guide to your work to-

©Andy Dean Photography/
shutterstock.com

Image Description: A traffic sign with the words "Do something" written on it.

ward making meaning in your life. Space has been provided for you to write in your own questions. It is important to remember that this is your journey and these questions are suggestions for prompts to your thinking. If they do not serve you, add your own so that this is meaningful and takes you a step forward in your life journey.

Guided Journaling Activity

For this exercise, you will need to find a comfortable and quiet place to write, free from distractions. Let your mind settle into a creative space where your answers can be free flowing and do not need to meet any particular criteria. Read the following questions and freely write whatever comes to your mind. Let the process evolve and your thoughts flow until you feel you have found a comfortable place to end, then move on to the next question.

1. My favorite way to spend the day is…
2. What does unconditional love mean to you? Look like to you?
3. Things I wish people knew about me or understood more about me…
4. Describe things or moments that bring you joy.
5. Write the words you need to hear.

"Let go of who you think you're supposed to be and embrace who you are."—Brene Brown

"Energy flows where intention goes"—Author Unknown

"Live more from intention and less from habit"—Amy Rubin Flett

"Live with intention. Walk to the edge. Listen hard. Practice wellness. Play with abandon. Laugh. Choose with no regret. Appreciate your friends. Continue to learn. Do what you love. Live as if this is all there is."—Mary Anne Radmacher

"The key question to keep asking is, are you spending your time on the right things?"—Randy Pausch

"You only live once, but if you do it right, once is enough."—Mae West

"Joy is not in things; it is in us."—Robert Wagner

"Joy does not simply happen to us. We have to choose joy and keep choosing it every day."—Henri J.M. Nouwen

"Joy is a decision, a really brave one, about how you are going to respond to life."—Wess Stafford

Gratitude

Now that we have discussed making meaning and finding joy, let's explore the concept of gratitude. Gratitude is a state of mind that arises when you affirm a good thing in your life or when you notice and enjoy little pleasures (Emmons & Stern, 2013). It is an expression of appreciation for what you have and a thoughtful acknowledgment of what you are thankful for. This is not just using polite manners and being sure to say "thank you" to others. Rather, heartfelt gratitude, the kind that can have a meaningful impact on your well-being, comes from intentional and mindful awareness of meaningful things in your life. Emmons and Stern (2013) found that gratitude is

Image Description: A photo of a piece of paper in a typewriter with the word "Gratitude."

©Mohd KhairilX/shutterstock.com

strongly linked to mental health and life satisfaction, stating, "There is a potent, vitalizing energy that accompanies both the affirmation and recognition components of gratitude and helps account for its transformational healing power in human functioning" (p. 847).

An article published by *Psychology Today* on gratitude goes on to say, "This proactive acknowledgment can increase well-being, health, and happiness. Being grateful, and especially the expression of it, is also associated with increased energy, optimism, and empathy." There are many benefits to practicing gratitude on a regular basis. It can help one sustain a more positive mindset, increase empathy and appreciation for others, and motivate positive change.

Three Forms of Gratitude (McCullough, Tsang, & Emmons, 2004).

1. Gratitude as **an (affective) trait**: A built in, personality level trait that determines how often and deeply we feel gratitude

2. Gratitude as **a mood**: Gratitude as a singular emotion lasts for only a few seconds. To explain how gratitude-inducing interventions like a gratitude journal work, rather than changing our personality trait, they instead induce a mood of gratitude, which in turn gives rise to more gratitude emotions.

3. Gratitude as **an emotion**: The actual positive emotions that recognize the intentional, beneficial actions of others—lasts only a few seconds.

Four Dimensions of Gratitude (McCullough, Emmons, & Tsang, 2002).

■ **Intensity:** The depth of the feeling, from a slight emotional tug to overflowing tears.

■ **Frequency:** The ease with which grateful feelings are elicited.

■ **Span:** The number of different things for which a person can be grateful for at the same time.

■ **Density:** The number of different people for which a person can be grateful for a single positive outcome.

Emmons and Stern (2013) found that, gratitude is not just a feeling that arrives arbitrarily. It is something you can choose at any time to tune into.

Gratitude promotes more gratitude. The process of intentionally integrating gratitude into your life triggers positive feedback loops, which contribute to more gratitude and positivity and who wouldn't like a little more positivity in their life?

Now let's talk about how you might start to intentionally integrate gratitude into your life. First, the practice of gratitude starts with awareness. Too often, our lives are consumed with being busy...working long hours, technology, activities, school, social gatherings, and in many cases, this detracts from our ability to be present. In order to become more aware, actively take notice of what is going on around you. Is it a particularly beautiful day? Did someone show you an act of kindness? Did you have a meaningful conversation with someone recently? There are an abundance of things throughout each day (big and little) that we can be grateful for, IF we are paying attention. Keep in mind that gratitude doesn't only apply to pleasant moments. We must also be mindful of moments that challenge us because they can be integral to meaningful change and growth, and we must be grateful for those as well.

Next, consider taking note of your gratitude in a more formal way. Writing things down can create a concrete account of our awareness and experiences. This will help to organize your thoughts and create a gratitude log that you can revisit and reflect on along the way. Just as you are probably more focused and successful in completing tasks when you have a written "to-do" list, you will be able to be more focused and successful practicing gratitude if you write it down regularly.

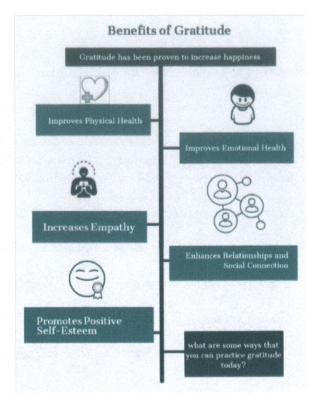

Image Description: A graphic describing the benefits of happiness.
Source: Bethany Novotny

Image Description: A photo of a cat laying in tall grass with the words "Be happy for this moment. This moment is your life."

In one study, people randomly assigned to keep weekly gratitude journals exercised more regularly, reported fewer physical symptoms, felt better about their lives, and were more optimistic about the upcoming week compared with people assigned to record hassles or neutral events. In another, young adults who kept a daily gratitude journal reported higher alertness, enthusiasm, determination, attentiveness, and energy compared with those who focused on hassles or compared themselves with others less fortunate (Emmons, Stern, & Stern, 2013).

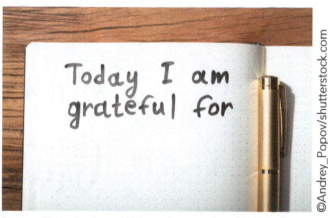

Image Description: Photo of a notebook and a pen with the words "Today I am grateful for..."

Finally, **communicating** gratitude completes the feeling of connection. Sometimes it is helpful just to acknowledge the gratitude out loud, even if you aren't stating your gratitude directly to someone. For example, each night after work, my partner and I share our "highlights and lowlights" from the day. Not only does this give us a chance to connect as a couple but we are intentionally bringing awareness to things in our day that we can be grateful for. Also, in the process of sharing this with my partner, I am always grateful for the active listening and attentiveness she shows me when we are in those moments. Remember, gratitude promotes more gratitude.

I'm sure that you can think of at least a handful of people who have played a significant role in your life. Maybe at the time, you didn't get the opportunity to truly thank them for the impact they had or maybe you didn't see how much they influenced you until much later on in your life. There are also ways to express gratitude for things that don't involve other people and that may be as simple as a moment of deliberate reflection.

Start your gratitude journey by committing to 7 days of gratitude. Keep in mind that the first few times you write you might not enjoy it, might not find it helpful, or might experience feelings that you didn't expect but don't let that discourage you. These are normal reactions to integrating a new practice in mindful reflection and it is important to recognize that as part of the experience. For the next 7 days keep a journal and write about the following:

Day 1: A list of what I am grateful for
Day 2: Gratitude for what went well today
Day 3: Three people I am grateful for and why
Day 4: List 10 hobbies or activities that bring you joy
Day 5: Write about a mistake that you've made that ultimately led to a positive experience or personal growth
Day 6: The biggest lesson you learned in childhood
Day 7: What is something you've learned this week that you are grateful for?

Want to keep writing? Feel free to come up with your own prompts or search online for "gratitude prompts" to continue your guided gratitude journey.

Activity/Homework

Write a Letter of Gratitude

Call to mind someone still alive who did something or said something that changed your life for the better; Someone you never properly thanked. Have someone in mind?

©Volvio/shutterstock.com

Image Description: Illustration of the words
"Practice gratitude" on a pastel background

Now write a letter of gratitude to this individual using the following pointers:

- Address the person directly ("Hello _____.").
- Be concrete. Describe what this person did for you. How did it affect your life? Why are you grateful to them/for them?
- Let the person know what you're doing now and mention how you often remember what they did.
- Include any additional information you want them to know.
- Aim for approximately 300 words.

Finding Yourself in the Service of Others

"The best way to not feel hopeless is to get up and do something. Don't wait for good things to happen to you. If you go out and make some good things happen, you will fill the world with hope, you will fill yourself with hope."

Barack Obama

We have discussed making meaning, finding joy, and developing gratitude—all tasks we do for ourselves. Now, let's turn our attention to what we can do for others. In a children's story about a lion and a mouse, service to others is highlighted. In this story, a sleeping lion is awakened by a tiny mouse. As the lion prepares to eat the mouse, the mouse begs him to spare him. "I may be of use to you one day", the mouse says. The lion looked at the small stature of the mouse and snorted, "how could you be of use to me!?" But, he reconsidered and let the mouse flee. No more than a few days later, the lion was caught in a trap. As he lamented his fate, the tiny mouse arrived and began to chew the rope that was binding the

©K. Jensen/shutterstock.com

Image Description: Illustration of a lion caught in a net with a mouse nearby lion. When the lion gained freedom, he thanked the mouse and realized **that no act of kindness or mercy is ever wasted!**

In today's world, we may be often confronted with acts of violence and feelings of despair. It can become very difficult to see the good that surrounds us. Mr. Fred Rogers (Mr. Roger's Neighborhood) recalled that when he was a little boy, he often became scared when bad things happened. When he was afraid, his mother would sit him down and tell him to "look for the helpers" during a crisis. This changed his viewpoint dramatically and from that point on, whenever he became afraid, he always focused on those that were there to help—it brought him comfort (Television Academy Foundation, 1999).

The act of helping others can be transformative—both for the person being helped and the person doing the helping. For some, service to others is a professional career—police officers, firemen, ministers, teachers, and health care workers are among the many. Their jobs involve providing needed services to others and many do so with a joyful heart. Others serve in a less formal way, responding to the needs of others in acute and chronic situations, without formal training and with selfless dedication. For our discussion on service, we will focus on the altruistic, informal service that any individual can undertake in their daily lives.

First, let's think about the people in your life who have helped you along the way. Parents, grandparents, teachers, coaches, mentors, siblings—the list goes on and on. Where might you be if you had not had help? How different might your life be? Now, think about those individuals that you have helped during your lifetime. How might you have changed their lives for the better? Did you see the outcome of your act of kindness? How did that make you feel? The fact of the matter is that helping others can often feel just as good for the helper as the helped. In fact, research studies have shown that helping others packs many benefits!

Benefits of Serving Others

So, what are some of the benefits? Let's see! According to MentalFloss.com (2019):

1. **HELPING OTHERS CAN HELP YOU LIVE LONGER.**
   You just might extend your lifespan! Research indicates that volunteering and acts of kindness can improve health in ways that can lengthen your lifespan—people who volunteered showed an enhanced ability to manage stress and avoid disease as well as exhibiting reduced rates of depression and an increased sense of life satisfaction—when volunteering on a regular basis. Volunteering has also been shown to alleviate loneliness and enhance our social lives—factors that can significantly affect our long-term health.

2. **HELPING OTHERS IS CONTAGIOUS**
   Researchers found that individuals are more likely to engage in altruistic acts after observing someone else perform a kindness. This chain reaction can create a ripple effect!

3. **HELPING OTHERS CAN MAKE US HAPPY**
   A team of sociologists reported that Americans who described themselves as "very happy" volunteered at least 5.8 hours per month. This improved sense of well-being could be the result of the physical benefits of volunteering but it may also be linked to increased feelings of social inclusion. There is even evidence that certain neurochemicals in the brain are positively affected by acts of altruism (Meier & Stutzer, 2008).

4. **HELPING OTHERS MAY HELP WITH CHRONIC PAIN.**
   A study by Arnstein, Vidal, Wells-Federman, Morgan, and Caudill (2002) indicated that individuals with chronic pain reported less symptoms and less intensity of symptoms while volunteering as a peer assistant to others in chronic pain. In addition, decreases in depression were also reported.

5. **HELPING OTHERS LOWERS BLOOD PRESSURE/CARDIOVASCULAR DISEASE RISK.**
   In another study done in 2013, volunteering was correlated with lowered blood pressure in older individuals (Sneed & Cohen, 2013). Individuals over the age of 50 who volunteered 200 hours or more a

year decreased their blood pressure readings by 40%! Additionally, Schreier, Schonert-Reichl, and Chen (2013) reported that adolescents who volunteered in their communities were more likely to have healthy hearts than their counterparts who did not volunteer.

Can you think of additional benefits of helping others?

6. **HELPING OTHERS GIVES US A SENSE OF PURPOSE AND SATISFACTION.**

Many studies have shown that volunteering increases one's sense of purpose and positively affects satisfaction with life, particularly for those individuals who no longer occupy a "service" role such as parent or grandparent.

Framing Service as A Core Value in Your Life

Clearly, there are several benefits for you as you help others! Not to mention the benefit you have provided to the person you are helping. Acts of caring can be done each day as opportunity arises—it doesn't always have to be planned. In fact, some of the most critical opportunties to help others take place unexpectedly—perhaps you see a motorist stranded on the side of the road or your next-door neighbor needs a last minute sitter. These opportunities arise frequently and could be chances to exercise our altristic muscles. Whether you practice service in a more formal way such as volunteering regularly, or more often respond to acute needs of those around you, service can become a lifestyle—a core value in your life.

In an article written by Taylor Pearson (n.d.), author of the *End of Jobs*, he identifies important steps in developing a core value. The process begins with agency. Let's take a closer look.

1. **"Agency:** to choose how I live and behave and help others do likewise; to be self-supportive and choose my own way of doing things."
2. **"Self-Development:** to keep growing, advancing, or improving in knowledge, skills, character, or life experience."
3. **"Courage:** to be courageous or brave; to persist in the face of fear, threat, or difficulty; to take risks for others."
4. **"Impact:** to exert myself into the universe in a way I believe is important. I work for what I want, not what others want from me."
5. **"Soul in the Game:** I believe it is an ethical concern that I put my money and time where my mouth is, that I have no divorce between what I preach and my lifestyle. I believe the highest form of ethics is to take on risk for others."
6. **"Reciprocity:** to create more value than I capture."

When applied to service to others, considering these steps can be helpful. In the first step, you are asked to evaluate the power of your own existence and how that power can be utilized to increase well-being for others. This is significant because it speaks to your ability to enact change through deliberate action on your part. You CAN make a difference. In the next step, you commit to a growth mindset, embracing learning opportunities (as well as service opportunities), to improve yourself so that you may be of better service to others. Acts of kindness often take courage. Sometimes the circumstances can be daunting, even dangerous. You may have doubts that you can even help. You may be

What stops you from helping others? Consider the possibilities.

embarrassed to offer your assistance. Yet, courage to step forward allows you to prevail. Deciding how you want to impact others' lives is also of paramount importance. Service to others is a choice. You are not required to do it. However, for many people helping others is integral to their self-concept and self-esteem. Additionally, how does your ethical code add up? Is service to others an essential part of your moral compass? Do you find yourself looking for opportunities to help others or avoiding other's needs? How does that impact your sense of self and your perception of your values? Finally, reciprocity as an act should be considered. Do you give as much as you get? Do you find yourself on the receiving end of assistance but rarely give back in return? If so, this may be a source of mental discomfort that you maybe had not even recognized before.

So, where do we start? We know that volunteerism is highly beneficial and there are a myriad of opportunities in your community to serve if you take a bit of time to explore. But remember, you don't always have to plan an opportunity to serve (although that is certainly admirable). Opportunities to serve may find you! You must first decide what is doable for you. Perhaps you work long hours or attend school most days of the week. You may not feel like you have the opportunity to volunteer many hours due to other responsibilities. That's okay! Not everyone can devote that kind of time; however, consider this—are there areas in your life where you *could* carve out a few hours to assist others. While it is vitally important that you have down time, perhaps you find yourself with more downtime than you actually need. Time spent watching television, surfing the internet, or interacting with social media might be an opportunity to get out in the community and assist. It is all about balance!

There are a myriad of opportunities to serve and it is very likely that you can find a way to serve that is also enjoyable for you. For example, perhaps you like to cook. You may identify an elderly neighbor who would love a home-cooked meal and take it to her once a month. Maybe you enjoy working with children. You could organize a new toy drive for a local pre-school. Perhaps you want to volunteer but don't have transportation. You can still help by recording books on tape for the blind or elderly. The only limit to how you can help is your imagination!

Once you have decided how you may be of service—get on out there and start! Remember, there are no "have-to's". You get to decide how you want to impact others and the manner in which you do it. Whatever you choose, it is likely that you will find a part of yourself that you didn't know existed, and when you do, you might be pleasantly surprised and find fulfillment that you didn't even know you was missing.

Image Description: Illustration of people constructing the word "Volunteer."

Identifying Your Service Preferences Activity

Identify A Population(s) That You Enjoy Working With

1. I enjoy interacting with:

   a. Infants and Toddlers   _____

   b. Elementary aged children   _____

   c. Adolescents   _____

   d. Elderly   _____

   e. Individuals with disabilities   _____

   f. Young adults   _____

   g. Middle-aged individuals   _____

   h. Other _____

Identify A Setting That You Might Enjoy Working In

2. I might enjoy working in:

   a. Court system
      - Legal Aide   _____

      - CASA (court appointed special advocate)   _____

   b. Community Organizations

      - Disability Services   _____

      - Domestic Violence   _____

      - Child Abuse   _____

   c. Community Service

      - Volunteer Fire Department   _____

      - Neighborhood Watch   _____

      - Neighborhood Initiatives   _____

   d. Food Service

      - Meals on Wheels   _____

   e. Nursing Home   _____

   f. Child-care   _____

   g. Boards of Directors for Non-Profits   _____

   h. Healthcare

      - Hospitals   _____

      - Local health departments   _____

    i. Arts

       ■ Art Guilds   _____

       ■ Community theatre   _____

       ■ Music instruction/chorale   _____

    j. Other_____

Identify Tasks/Skills That You Possess Or Want To Develop

3. I might like to work with/have skills in:

    a. Clerical (office assistance, copying, filing)   _____

    b. Advocacy   _____

       ■ Rallies, events   _____

       ■ Individual advocacy   _____

    c. Public Speaking   _____

    d. Organization (setting up systems)   _____

    e. Fund raising   _____

    f. Direct care (working directly with clients)   _____

    g. Grant writing   _____

    h. Transportation   _____

    i. Food Service (cooking, delivery)   _____

    j. Other _____

4. The hours that I can work during the week/month/year?

5. Locations that I am interested in volunteering?

6. Skills required for position of interest?

7. How will my volunteerism benefit those that I serve?

8. How will my volunteerism benefit me?

End of Chapter Self-Reflection

It's time to reflect on what you have learned about yourself through this chapter. Respond to each open-ended prompt on the staircase and save your answers for the culminating planning session at the end of the course.

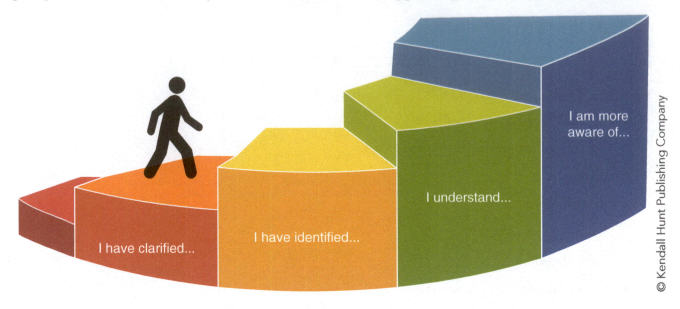

References

Arnstein, P., Vidal, M., Wells-Federman, C., Morgan, B., & Caudill, M. (2002). From chronic pain patient to peer: Benefits and risks of volunteering. *Pain Management Nursing, 3*(3), 94–103.

Emmons, R. A., Stern, D., & Stern, R. (2013). Gratitude as a psychotherapeutic intervention. *Journal of Clinical Psychology, 69*(8), 846–855.

McCullough, M. E., Emmons, R. A., & Tsang, J. (2002). The grateful disposition: A conceptual and empirical topography. *Journal of Personality and Social Psychology, 82*(1), 112–127. doi:10.1034//0022-3514.82.1.112

McCullough, M. E., Tsang, J., & Emmons, R. A. (2004). Gratitude in intermediate affective terrain: Links of grateful moods to individual differences and daily emotional experience. *Journal of Personality and Social Psychology, 86*(2), 295–309. doi:10.1037/0022-3514.86.2.295

Meier, S., & Stutzer, A. (2008). Is volunteering rewarding in itself? *Econimica, 75*, 39–59.

MentalFloss.com. (2019). 7 scientific benefits of helping others. Retrieved from http://mentalfloss.com/article/71964/7-scientific-benefits-helping-others

Pearson, T. (n.d.). How to discover your core values list (and use them to make better decisions). Retrieved from https://taylorpearson.me/core-values-list/

Schreier, H., Schonert-Reichl, K., & Chen, E. (2013). Effect of volunteering on risk factors for cardiovascular disease in adolescents. *JAMA Pediatrics, 167*(4), 327–332.

Schuback, A. (2019). Read the stories of 40 incredible kids who changed the world. Good Housekeeping. Retrieved from https://goodhousekeeping.com/life/inspirational-stories/g5188/kids-who-changed-the-world

Sneed, R. S., & Cohen, S. (2013). A prospective study in volunteerism and hypertension risk in older adults. *Psychology and Aging, 28*(2), 578–586.

Television Academy Foundation (Producer). (1999, July 22). Fred Rogers [Video file]. Retrieved from http://www.interviews.televisionacademy.com/interviews/fred-rogers

CHAPTER 4
Social Understanding and Engagement: Celebrating the Diversity Within Us All

©Felipe Teixeira/shutterstock.com

Image Description: A photo of a large crowd of people

In this chapter social awareness and engagement is explored. In a world where collaboration and cooperation is a central tenant, understanding and interacting effectively with others is paramount. Becoming more aware of others' cultures, needs and values can allow us to become more adept at building relationships and achieving goals through teamwork.

In this chapter, you will

- Learn to respond quickly and positively to others who are different from you
- Develop increased empathy and understanding of opportunities for advocacy for others
- Explore your own vulnerabilities and fears as it relates to "otherness"

Critical Skill Development: By cultivating these skills, you are opening yourself up to new experiences and people which can enrich your life in a myriad of ways. You may also increase your work potential in the field of your choice by being able to relate to a wider variety of individuals.

Cultural Diversity Self-Assessment

Prior to beginning the lesson on Cultural Competence, please complete the Cultural Diversity Self-Assessment. After completing the assessment, use the table below to create a plan to enhance your ability to successfully work with diverse individuals.

Scan the QR code to access the Cultural Diversity Self-Assessment

Cultural Diversity Self-Assessment Plan

No matter where your score falls on the Diversity Self-Assessment, remember that cultural competence is a journey and not necessarily a destination. We all have biases and prejudices that we must confronted in order to become more culturally competent.

GOAL DESCRIPTION	INTENDED RESULTS OR OUTCOMES	COMPLETION TIMELINE	RESOURCES IDENTIFIED	POSSIBLE ROADBLOCKS

©Benjavisa Ruangvaree Art/shutterstock.com

Image Description: An illustration of two heads back to back joined by a sun and surrounded by flowers and stars

Understanding Cultural Diversity and Multiculturalism

What is diversity and multiculturalism and why it is important?

Our world is more connected and our opportunity to interact and engage with many, many different types of people is greater than it has ever been. From supporting communities across the globe in recovering from natural disasters to advocating for the rights of others, our connectivity has brought more opportunity to share understandings with each other. With this access to so many cultures of people and diversity of thought, it is important that in those advocacy and support efforts, we are informed. The cyber world has offered us global connection and with that connection comes responsibility.

Becoming a support, ally, advocate, rescuer, friend—means we need to understand each other so that we can coexist respectfully and empathically. The work you will undertake in this next chapter hopes to take you to the next step in your journey of multicultural awareness and understanding. That understanding begins with your own self-identifiers and the awareness of how your background shapes your worldview. First, we will better understand what culture is then you will have the opportunity to answer some questions that may help you to conceptualize what is important in your culture of origin.

Culture refers to the shared language, beliefs, values, norms, behaviors, and material objects that are passed down from one generation to the next.

   a.   Patterns of human activity manifested in music, literature, lifestyle, customs, morals, beliefs, etc.
   b.   All the behaviors, ways of life, arts, beliefs, and institutions that are passed down from generation to generation
   c.   Spiritual, material, intellectual, and emotional features of a society or group

Reflect on your family/cultural background and then answer the following questions:

1.   What type of art or décor was displayed, appreciated, or enjoyed?

2.   What kind of music was enjoyed?

3.   What kind of music was criticized or forbidden?

4.   What foods were enjoyed?

5. What religious beliefs were practiced or encouraged?

6. What values were encouraged?

7. What type of clothing was worn?

8. What lifestyle was lived or aspired to?

9. What were some of the holiday celebrations/traditions in your family?

10. What messages about work and career did you receive?

11. What subcultures were you involved with?

12. What do you know about your family's ethnic background/heritage?

"**Multiculturalism** is a system of beliefs and behaviors that recognizes and respects the presence of all diverse groups in an organization or society, acknowledges and values their socio-cultural differences, and encourages and enables their continued contribution within an inclusive cultural context which empowers all within the organization or society" (Rosado, 2010).

Cultural diversity is a combination of all the things that make us unique as individuals and groups. Examples include ethnicity, language, age, religion, race, gender, sexual orientation, and so on. Cultural diversity supports the idea that every person can make a unique and positive contribution to the larger society because of, rather than in spite of, their differences. It helps dispel negative stereotypes and personal biases about different groups. In addition, cultural diversity helps us recognize and respect other "ways of being" that are not necessarily our own. As we interact with others, we can build bridges to trust, respect, and understanding across cultures (Belfield, 2012).

Image Description: An illustration of many different kinds of people smiling

Image Description: An illustration of many different kinds of people working together

Intent < Impact

When someone is hurt or offended, it is often unintentional or due to a lack of education or awareness around complex sociocultural factors. Typically, our initial reaction when we hurt or offend someone is to respond, "But I didn't mean it that way!" When someone does something hurtful or offensive to another person, the speaker's intent is not what's most important when gauging the appropriateness of an action. It may even be more harmful to redirect the focus of a conversation back to the speaker's presumably harmless intentions, rather than focusing on the **feelings** and **experiences** of the person who has been harmed. So, the point is that we really need to focus on *impact*, not intent. Was someone hurt by something? Was there a negative outcome? Did someone suffer? If so, that is what's important.

Being culturally competent means owning our mistakes. Sometimes, no matter how hard we try to be mindful of our speech and actions, we are bound to slip up and say something that hurts another person. Instead of minimizing that person's experience of being hurt, we should be empathetic and learn from the feedback that they offer. That is the best way to really enhance our cultural competence and grow. It's not easy, but it's worth it.

Tolerance < Affirmation and Celebration

It is not enough to just tolerate others. If you knew that someone only tolerated your existence instead of appreciating and loving you, it would not feel very good. Every human deserves equal affirmation and deserves to be appreciated for that which makes us unique.

When we celebrate the characteristics that make each of us unique, we imply that differences are not only natural, they are welcome! When varying voices are invited to the table, creativity abounds, problem-solving strategies

©Gustavo Frazao/shutterstock.com

Image Description: An illustration of a human handwriting the word "Discrimination"

©arloo/Shutterstock.com

may increase, and growth (both individual and group) occurs. As we move toward celebration and inclusion, our lives can be enriched by the experience of others. Celebrating our differences and similarities enables us to increase productivity in our workplaces, increase our circle of friends and build lasting community ties.

What happens when we don't appreciate and accept the diversity of others?

Prejudice: an unjustified or incorrect attitude (usually negative) toward an individual based solely on the individual's membership of a social group. Prejudice is often based on the inaccurate, incomplete, or generalized stereotype knowledge of a group.

Microaggressions are brief and commonplace daily verbal, behavioral, or environmental indignities, whether intentional or unintentional, that communicate hostile, derogatory, or negative prejudicial slights and insults toward any group, particularly marginalized groups (Peirce, 1970; Sue et al., 2007).

Has someone ever said something that hurt your feelings, but it was not their intention to hurt you? Microaggressions are similar in that way. It is important to understand that a lot of times people who engage in microaggressions will not believe that what they said was problematic, so calling them racist or sexist or homophobic would make them very defensive and make them unable to even recognize what their impact was.

We're all human. We are bound to make mistakes and we might commit microaggressions. It is not necessarily that you're a bad person if you commit a microaggression, but rather that you need to be more aware of your biases and impact on people. We all need to commit to working on these things in order to become more culturally competent.

Some examples of microaggressions are included below. Please write down what you think is wrong with each statement or how it might have a negative impact even if that was not the intent of the speaker.

- Telling a person of color, "You speak good English" or "you're so articulate."
- Asking a person of color, "where are you *really* from?" or "where were you actually born?"
- Telling a woman, "You should smile more."
- Mistaking a person of color for a service worker
- Asking a same sex couple, "So who is the man in the relationship?"
- A White man or woman clutching their purse or checking their wallet as a person of color approaches or passes.
- Telling a person of color, "When I look at you, I don't see color."
- Finding out someone has a mental health diagnosis and saying, "You have a mental illness, but you seem so normal."

 Scan the QR code to watch the video "Eliminating Microaggressions the Next Level of Inclusion" by Tiffany Alvoid

 Scan the QR code to explore more examples of common microaggressions.

Discrimination: the unjust or prejudicial behavior or actions, usually negative, toward an individual or group of people, especially on the basis of sex/race/social class, etc. Examples of common forms of discrimination:

- Harassment (inappropriate jokes, bullying, etc.)
- Wage discrimination (pay gap)
- Hiring practices
- Sex discrimination (pink tax, pregnancy discrimination)
- Housing (landlord that won't build an accessible ramp after tenant's injury)

Can you think of other examples of discrimination?

Prejudice can lead to discrimination, but it is not the only factor in discrimination. A person can harbor prejudices without discriminating, especially if they are mindful of their own prejudice and take proactive steps to counteract it.

Discrimination can lead to **oppression,** which is the unfair or cruel use of power to control another person or group. The term is often used in a political context to refer to the oppression of minority groups such as women and racial minorities. Slavery, the refusal to allow women to inherit and own property, the denial of equal rights to people with disabilities, and the involuntary commitment of people who deviate from social norms are all examples of oppression (Cudd, 2006).

Prejudice, discrimination, and oppression can all have major impacts on individuals and groups. Some of the common outcomes associated with experiencing prejudice, discrimination, and/or oppression include:

- Depression and anxiety.
- Impostor syndrome: the belief that one is inferior to or not as capable as others.
- Stereotype threat (Self-fulfilling prophecy): stereotype threat is the anxiousness that one feels about confirming a negative stereotype. This anxiousness can lead to actually confirming the negative stereotype, which would then be a self-fulfilling prophecy.

- Self-doubt. Prejudice is often subtle and comes in the form of microaggressions. Victims of prejudice and discrimination may question their perceptions of prejudice; perpetrators may encourage this self-doubt.

- Loss of opportunities. Prejudice that leads to discrimination deprives victims of opportunities and subjects them to more challenges than their peers. For instance, a black person at an elite school may have to work harder than a white peer to be taken seriously. Upon graduating, they may be paid less for the same work.

To reduce prejudice, we must create a culture where we accept and value the differences of others. It is important to note that when we truly value the diversity of others, we don't ask them to change or adopt the values of the dominant culture. Rather, we embrace how our differences can create a stronger and more authentic community. Additionally, it is important to realize that we do not have to agree on everything (or anything) to get along and respect one another. Respect is vital to creating a thriving diverse community, where people from all backgrounds and walks of life can live in community and be valued. The Cultural Civility Continuum is a visual aid that shows the varying degrees to which people accept or oppose diversity and the incorporation of diverse people into their communities.

Cultural Civility Continuum

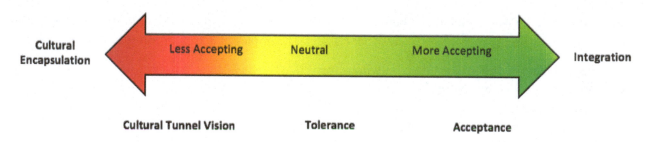

Image Description: Cultural Civility Continuum.
Source: Bethany Novotny

Cultural Encapsulation: a complete lack of understanding and appropriately responding to cultural differences in values, beliefs, perceptions, emotional responses, and behaviors. This mindset often consists of disinterest in other cultures and an active avoidance of cultural difference due to a monocultural belief system (belief in one "right" or superior culture).

Cultural Tunnel Vision: a limited capacity to recognize and respect cultural differences. It is often characterized by a variety of "cultural blind spots", having limited knowledge and/or exposure to different cultures, not considering or acknowledging how culture influences worldview, or an inability to recognize cultural differences based on an ethnocentric view.

Tolerance: Easily explained by the phrase, "go along to get along." Individuals who practice tolerance do not actively avoid cultural difference or reject its relevance, but they do not seek to better understand, recognize, or appreciate the value of diversity.

Acceptance: an intercultural approach that is characterized by recognizing and appreciating patterns of cultural difference and commonality in one's own and other cultures.

Integration: Embraces and celebrates diversity and multiculturalism in all forms. Recognizes the unique contributions that individuals from different cultural backgrounds can provide. Individuals who value integration seek to adapt to difference by shifting one's cultural perspective and by changing behaviors to exemplify authentic cultural sensitivity. This enables deep cultural bridging across diverse communities by navigating cultural commonalities and differences. Individuals who value cultural integration advocate for people to preserve their culture of origin (including languages, traditions, etc.) while being accepted and valued in the larger dominant culture, without being seen as an outsider or experiencing separation or marginalization.

Ethnocentric Monoculturalism:

"Ethnocentric (valuing of one's ethnic/cultural group over others) monoculturalism (belief in one "right" culture) is an unconscious or conscious overvaluation of one's own cultural beliefs and practices, and simultaneous invalidation of other cultural worldviews. In application, ethnocentric monoculturalism posits the individual's culture as normal and valid. Other cultures are viewed as abnormal, inferior, or pathological, with corresponding differential treatment" (Taylor, 2006, p. 204).

©Lightspring/shutterstock.com

Image Description: An illustration of multi-colored fingerprints

Privilege

In the realm of social justice, privilege is "a set of unearned benefits given to people who fit into a specific social group". The term "privilege", used in the context of social justice, can be traced back to the 1930s, when W.E.B. DuBois wrote about the "psychological wage" that allowed whites to feel superior to black people. Additionally, in the late 1980s, Peggy McIntosh discussed idea of privilege in a paper called "White Privilege and Male Privilege: A Personal Account of Coming to See Correspondences through Work in Women's Studies" as well as an article called "White Privilege: Unpacking the Invisible Knapsack", which first appeared in *Peace and Freedom* magazine.

Privilege is the opposite of oppression. It is made up of systems and social patterns, so we need to look at it systematically instead of individually to understand its impact. Having privilege doesn't mean that you are a bad person or that you are personally discriminating against or oppressing those with disadvantages; however, having privilege does provide unearned advantages. Privilege also doesn't mean that someone hasn't struggled. It is just likely that the areas where they experienced privilege wasn't the cause of their struggle. Also, we are all made up of multiple identities so one identity may give you privilege, while another is a disadvantage. For example, a poor white female has white privilege but is disadvantaged based on her socioeconomic status and gender. She has more privilege than a black poor woman who has multiple intersectional identities of oppression.

There is no blame in having privilege, only in failing to do something good with that privilege.

Scan the QR code to check out the TED talk, "The Power of Privilege" by Tiffany Jana

OR "Understanding My Privilege" by Sue Borrego

Equality < Equity

Knowing that privilege exists and is constantly influencing how people and systems operate leads us to discuss equality and equity. Equality, or treating everyone the same, seems like a good idea and it is definitely a step in the right direction; however, it misses a key point. Not everyone starts out with the same opportunities. Due to privilege, some individuals are disadvantaged before they even begin. Whether it is the color of someone's skin, the clothes they wear, their social standing, ability status, or anything else that can be considered a disadvantage in our society, the truth of the matter is that some people start with the cards stacked against them. Equality is not enough in these circumstances. Instead, we must strive for equity, or giving everyone what they need to succeed. In some cases, this might mean giving more to one person than another. It's not equal, but it levels the playing field. It is also important to note that we should never assume that we know what people need.

EQUALITY   EQUITY

"It is not our differences that divide us. It is our inability to recognize, accept, and celebrate those differences."
—Audre Lorde

©solarseven/shutterstock.com

Image Description: Four (4) people in bright colors jumping in celebration together

How can you practice becoming more culturally competent?

1. **Develop cultural self-awareness and sensitivity.** Through active self-reflection, we can understand our own identity and how we interact with the identity of others. Perhaps we discover that we are more accepting of some groups than others.

2. **Learn to appreciate, value, and celebrate diverse views.** Do not judge views that differ from yours as wrong. Embrace diversity of opinions, thoughts, and beliefs as multicolor fabrics sewn together to make a beautiful quilt.

3. **Avoid imposing your own values.** Be proactive in listening, valuing, and welcoming people and ideas that are different from your own.

4. **Resist stereotyping.** Stereotypes will always exist and come up, but recognize when you are stereotyping and avoid making generalizations about people based on those stereotypes.

5. **Learn what you can, whenever you can.** Be open to the stories and experiences of others. Increase your level of understanding about other cultures by interacting with people who are different from you.

6. **Accept your own naïveté.** Recognize that you don't know everything and never will. Instead of viewing this as a deficit, see it as an ongoing opportunity to learn.

7. **Strive for Equity.** Recognize when someone might need additional support in order to have the same opportunities.

8. **ACTION.** Intervene in an appropriate manner when you observe others engaging in behaviors that show cultural insensitivity, bias, or prejudice.

©Dietmar Temps/shutterstock.com

Cultural Responsiveness

An anthropologist proposed a game to the kids in an African tribe. He put a basket full of fruit near a tree and told them that whoever got there first won the sweet fruits. Then he gave them the signal to run and they all took each other's hand and ran together. They arrived at the basket and sat in a circle enjoying the sweet fruit together. When he asked them why they chose to run as a group when they could have had more fruit individually, one child spoke up and said, "UBUNTU, how can one of us be happy if all the others are sad?"

Developing cultural competence can have an impact on your personal and professional life. Being able to interact with others while acknowledging that we all come from different backgrounds and experiences helps us create more understanding and acceptance of others. Not being open to the difference of others can create a *fear response*. Fear is one instinctual way that our mind sends signals to keep us safe when we perceive a threat. Often, fear triggers the flight, fight, or freeze instinct, which is the physical and biochemical reaction to fear. This is a crucial response when it is a survival situation but when it comes to people who are different, we have been *taught* and *socialized* to fear "others".

When we are more in touch with the experiences of others, we are better able to express *empathy*, or feeling WITH someone, and to understand where they are coming from. It takes courage to be *vulnerable* with another human being. Being vulnerable means deconstructing barriers that have served as coping mechanisms or protective factors. To let our guard down means to take a great risk but with great risk, there is a possibility for great reward. Being vulnerable isn't always comfortable. In fact, it is quite uncomfortable. When we step outside our comfort zone, we provide ourselves the opportunity to experience that which is unfamiliar. We allow experiences to touch us more deeply and words to connect more meaningfully.

Three Parts of Empathy:

Perspective taking: put our own "stuff" aside and be fully present with another person	**Suspension of judgement:** not placing blame or shame on someone and not discounting their experience or feelings	**Emotional intelligence:** recognizing emotions in others and communicating that

Empathy: the ability to understand and share the feelings of another
Vulnerability: uncertainty, risk and emotional exposure

Sympathy < Empathy

Sympathy describes feeling sorry for someone. Empathy means feeling **with** someone. We are all human and we [humans] experience many of the same emotions throughout our lives. Empathy allows us to be present with someone and relate to their emotions, even if we are not currently experiencing the same emotions. For example, recently my brother and his wife came to visit with their two kids. We all went on a hike together and while on the hike, my sister-in-law became ill. My nephew was pestering her and pulling on her arm to try to gain her attention. I pulled him aside and asked him if he remembers a time when he felt sick and wanted to be left alone. He thought for a few moments then talked about a time when he was sick and spent the day home from school in his room. I asked if he expected people to be kind and sensitive to him when he wasn't feeling well and he agreed that was his expectation. By bringing his awareness to a common experience and common emotions, my nephew was able to be more empathetic with his mother. He was able to be more attentive to what she needed at the time rather than making his needs the focus.

Want to learn more? Watch this short video where Brene Brown explains the difference between sympathy and empathy and why it is important to understand. https://www.youtube.com/watch?v=1Evwgu369J

@arloo/ shutterstock.com

Image Description: Colorful heart with the word "Empathy" written across it

Interested in learning more? Consider exploring The 10 Lenses: Your Guide to Living and Working in a Multicultural World by Mark Williams

©Aleksandar Mijatovic/shutterstock.com

Image Description: An illustration of the human eye with the world map in the iris

Outside the "ZONE": Embracing Opportunities for Knowledge and Growth

We all should strive toward **cultural relativism,** which is the ability to understand a culture on its own terms and not to make judgements using the standards of one's own culture. The goal of this is to promote understanding of cultural practices that are not typically part of one's own culture.

Image Description: An illustration of a circle that is labeled "Comfort Zone" with an arrow pointing outside the circle to the words "Where the magic happens"

Image Description: A photo of two plants and a sign that says "Life begins at the end of your comfort zone"

©iQoncept/shutterstock.com

A lesson from Chaz Kellem

My name is Chaz Kellem and I identify as someone that is comfortable and proud with the skin I am in and appreciate all the identities that make me who I am. I am black. I am disabled. I am a husband. I am a coach.

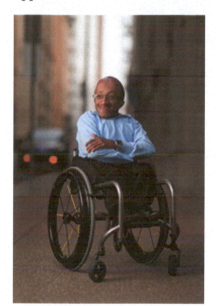

I am a friend. I am all of these and more. All these identities make me and have given me a unique perspective that I value. I am a person that accepted that I am uniquely motivated by the simple pleasures of life—each moment. Appreciating the past, respecting our current place and paying attention to our potential for growth, inspires and motivates me.

I was born with osteogenesis imperfecta, which is a rare bone disease that not only has impacted my life on a daily basis but will for certain influence my future. I have experienced over 40 broken bones and more than 10 operations. With this disorder, bones will break with little to no force. While my bones have strengthened over the years and available treatments have improved, there is currently no cure. I can and have done hard things throughout my life and this started very young. Around the age of seven, I decided to use a manual wheelchair full-time. Quality of life and happiness was the core of this decision. I certain did not recognize this then (as I wanted to simply play, laugh, and have fun) but I am grateful for that decision now.

As I embark on a new day and recognize how dynamic my life experience may appear, I am constantly reminding myself there is a great deal I do not know about people, places and things. I have befriended some amazing people and learned amazing lessons at some of the most unexpected times. The encouragement that I gather from the world is there remains a constant willingness to learn and an eagerness from some, to have tough discussions. I do not want to delude how tough talking about diversity, inclusion, equity, and cultural responsiveness can be, as it requires us to be vulnerable. I have faith—hope—and believe that we are better together and can make progress by working hard and 'practicing' unconditional positive regard, acceptance, and empathy daily.

I never want to be an after-school special or speak for an entire community. People will often ask about my legacy—which can be a complicated question. For years, it has and remains simple—and that is to leave things better than I found them. I hope to be appreciated for the true essence of the person I am… the friendships made, the lessons taught and learned, and the laughs shared. I appreciate the journey ahead, and simply have to smile (occasionally laugh), and the unknown future ahead. I am ready to tackle the future head-on as I continue to prepare, study, learn—Are You Ready?

Be open! Trust yourself! Be the exception to the rule. Listen to others. Have patience. Pause and smell the rain, look at the rainbow and forgive yourself. Love hard—and value those that may be different from you in various ways. Believe in the unbelievable on a daily basis. As you work through this book, I hope you find your way—bit by bit and MOMENT by MOMENT.

The Chaz Kellem Pledge

I pledge that I will begin to understand and embrace my full self, all my identities, and the identities of others through practicing unconditional positive regard, acceptance, and empathy. I will strive to live moment by moment, recognizing that the journey and all its moments are part of my growth. I will value and recognize that while I may be different than others—I also have many similarities and will commit to learn from the differences of others. I pledge to appreciate the moments passed, never allow someone to have power over me, and be thankful and grateful each day.

©hendra yuwana/shutterstock.com

X _____

End of Chapter Self-Reflection

It's time to reflect on what you have learned about yourself through this chapter. Respond to each open-ended prompt on the staircase and save your answers for the culminating planning session at the end of the course.

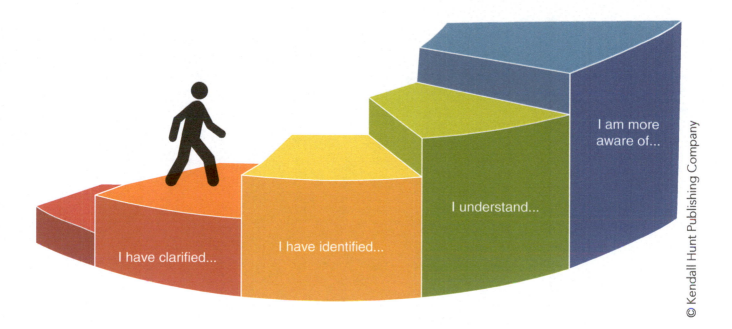

I have clarified...

I have identified...

I understand...

I am more aware of...

© Kendall Hunt Publishing Company

References

Brown, B. C. (2012). Daring greatly: How the courage to be vulnerable transforms the way we live, love, parent, and lead. New York, NY: Gotham.

Cudd, A. E. (2006). *Analyzing oppression.* New York, NY: Oxford University Press.

Heppner, P. P., Wang, K. T., Heppner, M. J., & Wang, L.-F. (2012). From cultural encapsulation to cultural competence: The cross-national cultural competence model. In N. A. Fouad, J. A. Carter, & L. M. Subich (Eds.), *APA handbooks in psychology: APA handbook of counseling psychology, Vol. 2. Practice, interventions, and applications* (pp. 433–471). Washington, DC: American Psychological Association. http://dx.doi.org/10.1037/13755-018

Sue, D. W., Capodilupo, C. M., Torino, G. C., Bucceri, J. M., Holder, A. M. B., Nadal, K. L., & Esquilin, M. (2007). Racial microaggressions in everyday life: Implications for clinical practice. *American Psychologist, 62*(4), 271–286. http://dx.doi.org/10.1037/0003-066X.62.4.271

Taylor, J. (2006). Ethnocentric monoculturalism. In Y. Jackson (Ed.), *Encyclopedia of multicultural psychology* (pp. 204–204). Thousand Oaks, CA: SAGE. doi:10.4135/9781412952668.n105

UNIT III

Personal Resources: Assets and Aptitudes

Image Description: A person drawing and coloring an elephant on a sheet of paper with coffee, pens, paper, and a plant nearby

©ABO PHOTOGRAPHY/shutterstock.com

The purpose of this unit is to explore what personal resources you have that you can tap into and identify those that you may wish to develop. We all have strengths but we don't always know how to harness them and use them to our advantage. This unit will help you identify your personal resources and strengths and identify some concrete ways to put them into action!

CHAPTER 5
Wellness Check

©Polarpx/shutterstock.com

Image Description: A photo of Scrabble tiles that spell the word "Wellness"

This chapter will highlight the need to "check in" with ourselves regularly to make sure that we are maintaining balance and optimal wellness. We all get caught up in our busy lives and it is easy for days or even weeks to slip by without realizing that we may need to take a breather. This chapter will provide a framework on how to stay mindful about your needs and self-care.

In this chapter you will:

- Learn the skills associated with critical thinking
- Develop an awareness of growth mindset
- Explore your assets and aptitudes using various personal exploration activities
- Increase your awareness of the importance of curiosity and lifelong learning

Critical skill development: To develop self-awareness and skills to strive toward optimal wellness, reduce stress, and ask for help, when needed.

Assessing Our Wellness

In our lives, we have all kinds of priorities, obligations, relationships, interests, and activities that compete for our time. We have the things that we must do, like going to school, going to work, caring for others, and paying bills. We also have things that we enjoy and make us happy, like spending time with family and friends, engaging in hobbies, or outdoor recreation like hiking or kayaking.

Balance means that we can fully engage in what we need or want to do without harboring guilt or worry that we should be doing something else. It means really understanding our own boundaries and needs so that we have the freedom to pursue all the various roles and identities we have or want to have in life. Finding balance leads to greater life satisfaction and well-being.

We all exert mental energy when we complete tasks so we need to be aware of how to best recharge and get back into balance. Balance is individualistic. Remember, there are a lot of different ways to find balance and not everyone finds it in the same way. I know that I need a lot more down time while my partner prefers to stay busy all the time. I need a lot of quiet time to reenergize while my partner gets energized from being around friends in a social setting. You may already know what works for you but if you don't, take some time to reflect on times when you feel most happy and at ease. Consider the following questions:

- When do I feel most energized?
- Does being around a group of people make me feel invigorated or drained?
- Does spending time by myself help me refocus?
- Do you consider yourself more of an intellectual person or emotional person?

One more thing to consider . . . **Are you an empath?** (Refer back to your personality typology in Chapter 1 here!) Empaths are highly sensitive individuals, who often have a heightened sense of awareness to their environment and have a keen ability to sense what people around them are feeling. It is important to identify if you are a highly sensitive person because you may need to attend to your emotional health more intentionally and more frequently than others. Find out more here: http://www.hsperson.com.

A big part of balance is deciding what tasks or activities are priorities and what tasks or activities can wait. Of course, there are things that we really must do—our bosses and professors expect us to complete work on time, and we need to eat and maintain a home to stay healthy, and we may provide care for others. The problem is that we often spend too much time on things we think that we must do that we neglect the things that make us feel happy and well. I have heard my students talk about skipping meals because they feel like they don't have time in the day to eat. When we are overwhelmed, what we often don't realize is that neglecting important things like food and self-care actually makes us function less effectively in other areas of our lives.

Tips for Balance at School

- Figure out how you like to work. Do you prefer to study at the library, with a group of friends, or at home?
- Set a schedule that includes all of your obligations and fun activities—and stick to it.
- Evaluate your week in advance. If it is going to be particularly busy, make sure you have snacks with you at all times so that you are not skipping meals.
- If you're feeling overwhelmed by an assignment, talk with your professor.
- See how your school can help—many offer help with studying strategies, planning, writing, and other areas.
- Join a group or club around something you enjoy—it can be fun and broaden your social networks.
- Try to start assignments early so unexpected problems or events won't be as difficult to work around.

Take a moment to recall the work we did at the end of Chapter 1 related to the Wellness Wheel and creating a healthy life balance. In this section, you will be able to assess yourself on each dimension of the wellness wheel to get a sense of areas of wellness you are attending to regularly and those areas that you may be neglecting. Remember, it is sometimes difficult or even impossible to attend to all areas of the wheel all the time. What is important is that you do not let one or more area remain unattended to for too long. Consider what areas of the wheel are easier for you to attend to. Perhaps the social dimension gets a lot of your attention because you prioritize fun activities and friend time. Does putting too much attention in the

©Dean Drobot/shutterstock.com

Image Description: A photo of a person meditating in an office chair

social dimension ever detract from your attention to schoolwork? As you assess each dimension of the wheel, consider what relationship the dimensions have with one another. It is a good idea to revisit the wellness wheel from time to time to reevaluate which areas of your life are getting a lot of attention and what areas you may not be attending to as well.

The Six Dimensions of Wellness Model

Developed by Dr. Bill Hettler, co-founder of the National Wellness Institute (NWI), this interdependent model, commonly referred to as the Six Dimensions of Wellness, provides the categories from which NWI derives its resources and services.

A Description of Each Dimension

OCCUPATIONAL

The occupational dimension recognizes personal satisfaction and enrichment in one's life through work. At the center of occupational wellness is the premise that occupational development is related to one's attitude about one's work. Traveling a path toward your occupational wellness, you'll contribute your unique gifts, skills, and talents to work that is both personally meaningful and rewarding. You'll convey your values through your involvement in activities that are gratifying for you. The choice of profession, job satisfaction, career ambitions, and personal performance are all important components of your path's terrain.

Occupational wellness follows these tenets:
- It is better to choose a career which is consistent with our personal values, interests, and beliefs than to select one that is unrewarding to us.
- It is better to develop functional, transferable skills through structured involvement opportunities than to remain inactive and uninvolved.

PHYSICAL

The physical dimension recognizes the need for regular physical activity. Physical development encourages learning about diet and nutrition while discouraging the use of tobacco, drugs and excessive alcohol consumption. Optimal wellness is met through the combination of good exercise and eating habits. As you travel the wellness path, you'll strive to spend time building physical strength, flexibility and endurance while also taking safety precautions so you may travel your path successfully, including medical self-care and appropriate use of a medical system. The physical dimension of wellness entails personal responsibility and care for minor illnesses and also knowing when professional medical attention is needed. By traveling the wellness path, you'll be able to monitor your own vital signs and understand your body's warning signs. You'll understand and appreciate the relationship between sound nutrition and how your body performs. The physical benefits of looking good and feeling terrific most often lead to the psychological benefits of enhanced self-esteem, self-control, determination and a sense of direction.

Physical wellness follows these tenets:
- It is better to consume foods and beverages that enhance good health rather than those which impair it.
- It is better to be physically fit than out of shape.

SOCIAL

The social dimension encourages contributing to one's environment and community. It emphasizes the interdependence between others and nature. As you travel a wellness path, you'll become more aware of your importance in society as well as the impact you have on multiple environments. You'll take an active part in improving our world by encouraging healthier living and initiating better communication with those around you. You'll actively seek ways to preserve the beauty and balance of nature along the pathway as you discover the power to make willful choices to enhance personal relationships and important friendships, and build a better living space and community.

Social wellness follows these tenets:
- It is better to contribute to the common welfare of our community than to think only of ourselves.
- It is better to live in harmony with others and our environment than to live in conflict with them.

INTELLECTUAL

The intellectual dimension recognizes one's creative, stimulating mental activities. A well person expands his or her knowledge and skills while discovering the potential for sharing his or her gifts with others. Using intellectual and cultural activities in the classroom and beyond the classroom combined with the human resources and learning resources available within the university community and the larger community, a well person cherishes intellectual growth and stimulation. Traveling a wellness path, you'll explore issues related to problem solving, creativity, and learning. You'll spend more time pursuing personal interests and reading books, magazines, and newspapers, while keeping abreast of current issues and ideas. As you develop your intellectual curiosity, you'll actively strive to expand and challenge your mind with creative endeavors.

Intellectual wellness follows these tenets:

- It is better to stretch and challenge our minds with intellectual and creative pursuits than to become self-satisfied and unproductive.
- It is better to identify potential problems and choose appropriate courses of action based on available information than to wait, worry, and contend with major concerns later.

SPIRITUAL

The spiritual dimension recognizes our search for meaning and purpose in human existence. It includes the development of a deep appreciation for the depth and expanse of life and natural forces that exist in the universe. Your search will be characterized by a peaceful harmony between internal personal feelings and emotions and the rough and rugged stretches of your path. While traveling the path, you may experience many feelings of doubt, despair, fear, disappointment and dislocation, as well as feelings of pleasure, joy, happiness and discovery. These are all important experiences and components to your search and will be displayed in the value system you will adapt to bring meaning to your existence. You'll know you're becoming spiritually well when your actions become more consistent with your beliefs and values, resulting in a "world view."

Spiritual wellness follows these tenets:

- It is better to ponder the meaning of life for ourselves and to be tolerant of the beliefs of others than to close our minds and become intolerant.
- It is better to live each day in a way that is consistent with our values and beliefs than to do otherwise and feel untrue to ourselves.

EMOTIONAL

The emotional dimension recognizes awareness and acceptance of one's feelings. Emotional wellness includes the degree to which one feels positive and enthusiastic about one's self and life. It includes the capacity to manage one's feelings and related behaviors including the realistic assessment of one's limitations, development of autonomy, and ability to cope effectively with stress. The well person maintains satisfying relationships with others. Awareness of, and accepting a wide range of feelings in yourself and others is essential to wellness. On the wellness path, you'll be able to express feelings freely and manage feelings effectively. You'll be able to arrive at personal choices and decisions based upon the synthesis of feelings, thoughts, philosophies, and behavior. You'll live and work independently while realizing the importance of seeking and appreciating the support and assistance of others. You'll be able to form interdependent relationships with others based upon a foundation of mutual commitment, trust, and respect. You'll take on challenges, take risks, and recognize conflict as being potentially healthy. Managing your life in personally rewarding ways, and taking responsibility for your actions, will help you see life as an exciting, hopeful adventure.

Emotional wellness follows these tenets:

- It is better to be aware of and accept our feelings than to deny them.
- It is better to be optimistic in our approach to life than pessimistic.

Applying the Six Dimensions of Wellness Model

By applying the model, a person becomes aware of the interconnectedness of each dimension and how they contribute to healthy living. This holistic model explains:

- how a person contributes to his or her environment and community, and how to build better living spaces and social networks;
- the enrichment of life through work, and its interconnectedness to living and playing;
- the development of belief systems, values, and creating a world-view;
- the benefits of regular physical activity, healthy eating habits, strength and vitality, as well as personal responsibility, self-care and when to seek medical attention;
- self-esteem, self-control, and determination as a sense of direction;
- creative and stimulating mental activities, and sharing your gifts with others.

Applying a wellness approach can be useful in nearly every human endeavor. As a pathway to optimal living, wellness is being applied to related fields, such as health promotion and holistic health, and has seen a growth in "helping professions" including counseling and medical arts and practices. The National Wellness Institute devised three questions that can help persons and organizations assess the degree to which wellness is incorporated into a particular approach or program:

- Does this help people achieve their full potential?
- Does this recognize and address the whole person (multi-dimensional approach)?
- Does this affirm and mobilize people's positive qualities and strengths?

Pause for Self-Reflection

Let's take a moment to revisit the wellness wheel. Think about each area of the wheel in the diagram below and take some time to write notes in each section. Include some positive affirmation in areas where you feel that you are excelling currently and include some notes to yourself on areas where you may need to spend more energy. Remember, wherever you are is fine. It is nearly impossible to attend to all the areas of your life simultaneously. Instead, seek a realistic balance. For example, you may need to be willing to give up some of your social freedom in order to focus on your emotional health and schoolwork right now. Don't be too hard on yourself. Acknowledge wins where you can and challenge yourself to take small steps in areas where you need to grow. When you are finished with the wheel, you may move on to the Life Balance Assessment and Action Planning Guide using the QR code below.

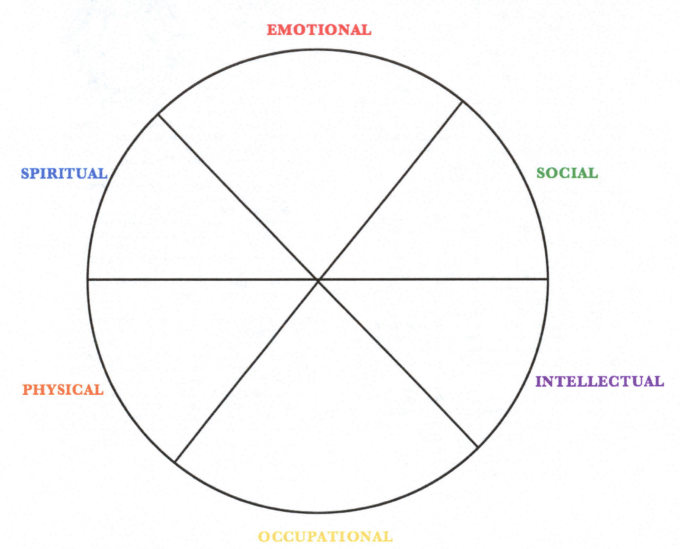

Image Description: Wellness Wheel
Source: Bethany Novotny

Scan the QR code to access the Life Balance Assessment and Action Planning Guide

Emotional Wellness and Self-Esteem

"Emotion is created by a cause, whether that cause is factual or imaginary does not matter, as long as the believer holds it as true."

Bangambiki Habyarimana

Image Description: Photo of a smooth, black rock with the word "Wellness" written across it

©Bildagentur Zoonar GmbH/shutterstock.com

We have learned about making meaning and finding joy, approaching life with gratitude, learning to live with intent, and achieving balance. All those things are important components to our sense of self and central to the concept of emotional wellness. Our emotions are complex and subject to change based on the circumstances we face and how we *interpret* those circumstances. What *we* see may not be what others see; however, our emotions spring from *our* perceptions of reality. Thus, thoughts and emotions are closely correlated.

Emotions allow us to express our feelings about our inner and outer environments. They are perfectly natural and instinctive. They guide us toward action or inaction and let us know when a situation is rewarding or untenable. But it is their relationship with our thoughts that is perhaps most interesting. Researchers Beck and Ellis (1976) formulated a theory based on this very partnership.

When was the last time your thoughts defeated you?

Our thoughts, emotions, and behaviors are cyclically interacting. These transactional interactions mean that all components (thoughts, emotions, and behaviors) are influencing each other constantly. For example, you may encounter a person that you like very much and you want to ask them out on a date, but you find that your thoughts are negative, "they won't like me or ever go out with me. Why try? They will just reject me." These negative thoughts produce negative emotions such as despair and feelings of hopelessness. In turn, the negative emotions that you are feeling lead you to act in a certain way—in this case, you don't approach your romantic interest and you don't ask them out. Then you feel bad about your decision and the cycle begins again. Thus, thoughts are central to the idea of emotional wellness. How we think determines how we behave!

Maladaptive thought patterns can get in our way. These *cognitive distortions* can lead us to a state of emotional discomfort. Let's explore some of the more common types of distortions.

- **Black/White Thinking**: This refers to either/or thinking, black or white. This type of thinking ignores the middle ground and all the shades of gray that lie between. This prevents one from considering other plausible possibilities.
- **Personalization**: When a person takes everything personally—assuming that one's or life circumstances are due to a defect in their personality rather than other relevant factors.
- **Should Statements**: "I should have lost weight", "I should have realized something was wrong", "He should have foreseen the consequences." These are all "should" statements. The words "should, ought, or must" are almost always linked to a cognitive distortion. This applies to how we judge others as well. Should statements often lead to feelings of guilt or shame and are frequently pointless.
- **Catastrophizing**: This happens when we only see the absolute worst outcome. For example, when you fail a test, you automatically assume you will fail the whole class.

- **Magnifying Negatives/Minimization of Positives:** This occurs when one overly focuses on the negative aspects of a situation, and chooses to ignore the positive aspects.
- **Mindreading:** When we assume the role of a psychic and believe that we know what others are thinking, even when there is no evidence to support our conjectures.
- **Fortune Telling:** When we predict something (usually negative) is going to happen without any evidence that a negative outcome is imminent.
- **Overgeneralization:** Often contains the words, "always, never, every, or all." This happens when we take one or two events and generalize them to the whole lot. For example, you run into a person that you know and wave but the person does not wave back. You react by saying "everybody hates me; nobody likes me."
- **Filtering:** This occurs when one filters out relevant information (positive or negative). This can often lead to increased focus on information that supports your point of view and decreased focus on data that does not support your conjecture.
- **Labeling:** Similar to overgeneralization, labeling is when you take one event (usually negative) and label yourself based on that event. An example might be that you strike out in a ballgame. You decide that it was not just mistake but that you are actually a "failure" at baseball.
- **Blaming:** Instead of seeing everything as your fault, you see it as entirely someone else's fault regardless of whether that is accurate or not.
- **Emotional Reasoning:** This occurs when you make decisions based entirely on your emotions (which may not be logical or rational).
- **Always Being Right:** When one believes that their opinions, etc. are always right, it prevents them from seeing the viewpoints of others and can make healthy relationships difficult.
- **Self-Serving Bias:** A person may attribute all positive outcomes to their own personal character while attributing negative outcomes to "things that they have no control over." This can prevent individuals from admitting when they are wrong and stifle emotional and psychological growth.
- **Fallacy of Change:** When a person believes their own happiness depends on others' actions or their ability to change.
- **Fallacy of Fairness:** This occurs when one expects everything to be fair and equitable when in reality that is not always possible.
- **Fallacy of Control:** A false sense of governance over others' actions, feelings, and thoughts.

When we use cognitive distortions (and sometimes this is beyond our awareness) we set ourselves up to feel badly. These unhealthy thought patterns prevent us from viewing situations realistically and rationally, which in turn affects our ability to make well-informed decisions.

How might you deal with intrusive negative thoughts?

So, if cognitive distortions are unhealthy, how do we arrest those patterns and replace them with healthier processes? Let's explore that together! CMHBC and Anxiety Canada (2016) offer a few solutions. First, it is probably not helpful to just tell yourself "stop thinking that way." By pushing thoughts away, you don't get the opportunity to examine evidence and challenge the "thinking trap." Also, thoughts pushed away often have a habit of coming back.

1. Try to separate your thoughts from actual events

Ask yourself the following questions when something distressing happens:

- What actually occurred? State only the facts—things everybody would agree that happened.
- What are you thinking? What are you telling yourself about the situation?
- What are your feelings? Do a gut check.
- How are your reacting to the situation? What are your behaviors and coping mechanisms?

2. Identify the cognitive distortion

Look particularly at your thoughts. Are you employing one or more cognitive distortions? It's common to fall into more than one thinking trap. From the list of cognitive distortions beginning on page 99, list the distortions you may be using.

3. Challenge the distortion

Now look at each trap as if you are studying it as scientist would. Be as objective as possible and try to challenge the trap using the following tools:

- **Examine the evidence**: Try to find evidence that refutes the trap! For example, if you make a parenting mistake, you may be thinking "I am a terrible parent! I never do anything right!" However, when you look at your child and find them to be well-behaved and mannerly, you have identified data that speaks to the contrary. In fact, you are not a terrible mom or dad—you just made a mistake and it doesn't define your entire worth as a parent.
- **Double-standard**: Harsh criticism of self is quite common. Ask yourself "would I judge someone else in the same situation as harshly?"
- **Survey Method**: Ask trusted friends and family their opinions. You may think "no other student has this problem." Yet, when you ask others their experiences, you often find that they have been through similar circumstances.
- **Conduct an experiment**: Test your beliefs! For example, if you think your friends are too busy for you, call them up and ask them to do something. You could find that they welcome the invitation!

SITUATION	THOUGHTS	DISTORTION/TRAP	CHALLENGE
My friend didn't come to my birthday party.	She is so rude! She doesn't like me anymore.	Labeling/Mind Reading	Examine the evidence: She has always been there for me in the past and we have not been upset with each other lately.

Replace with more balanced thought: She probably has a very good reason that she didn't come and will likely call me to let me know why when she can.

Image Description: An illustration of sign post with arrows pointing in different directions with the words "Elation, peace, glee, happy, ecstasy, rapture, bliss, delight, cheer, and joy written on them

©Ryan DeBeradinis/shutterstock.com

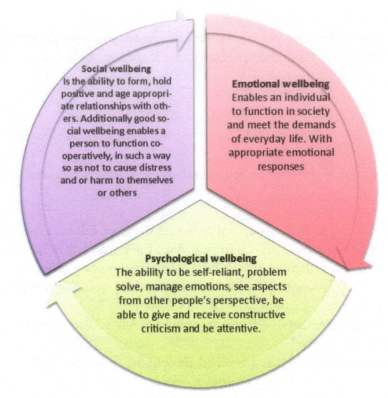

Social wellbeing
Is the ability to form, hold positive and age appropriate relationships with others. Additionally good social wellbeing enables a person to function cooperatively, in such a way so as not to cause distress and or harm to themselves or others

Emotional wellbeing
Enables an individual to function in society and meet the demands of everyday life. With appropriate emotional responses

Psychological wellbeing
The ability to be self-reliant, problem solve, manage emotions, see aspects from other people's perspective, be able to give and receive constructive criticism and be attentive.

From Social, Emotional, and Mental Health by Nick Millward.
Copyright © 2020 by CORNWALL.GOV.UK. Reprinted by permission.

4. Aim for balance in your thoughts

Now that you have clearly identified the thinking trap/distortion, try to replace it with a more balanced thought. Here is an example.

Of course there are times when negative thinking is called for and realistic. How do you cope during these instances? It may be helpful to try to find the learning opportunity that is almost always present during distressing times. What can you learn about yourself or others during this situation? What lesson can you learn to improve your future outlook? It may also help to concentrate on the coping mechanisms that you are choosing. Highlight healthy strategies and try to minimize negative ones. Repeat to yourself, "I am strong and I am healthy!"

Now let's talk about other ways to increase emotional wellness. Aside from recognizing and arresting cognitive distortions, what other tools might we use to ensure that we are psychologically healthy? The editors of FamilyDoctor.org (2017) provide a list of suggestions.

1. **Increase your awareness of your own emotions**. Learn to recognize situations that make your angry, sad, happy, or fulfilled. For those circumstances that make you feel negatively, develop a plan to try and change those situations in some way.
2. **Express your feelings appropriately/Think before you act**. Internalizing your feelings may not always be healthy. Find a trusted friend to share your feelings with or write in a journal. The important thing is to find a positive outlet for your feelings. Likewise, it may not always be appropriate to externalize your feelings if you are highly emotionally charged. It might be best to give yourself some extra time to distance yourself from these emotions so that you can see the situation more clearly.
3. **Learn to manage stress in your life**. We will not always be able to excise *all* of life's stressors but we can do our best to minimize situations that tend to distress us. Letting go of or reframing unhealthy

relationships is a strong first step. Be purposeful in choosing people and places that bring you joy. When stress cannot be avoided, make attempts to adopt healthy coping mechanisms that can ease your burden.

4. **Strive for balance**. Don't ever forget that life is a finely choreographed dance between work and play. When it is time to work, focus and give it 100% of your effort but when it is time for rest and relaxation—go at it with just as much gusto and don't feel guilty about it. Our brains and bodies require time to recharge in order to remain healthy.

5. **Take care of your physical health**. As the saying goes, a healthy mind follows a healthy body. Take time to exercise or do other physical activities that you enjoy! Eat well and take prescribed medications as directed. Take a walk, hike a trail or commune with nature if you enjoy being outdoors.

6. **Connect with others/nurture relationships**. It is vitally important for us to find connection with others in some way. Take care of your relationships and if you don't have connections with others, find a way to develop them. There are many opportunities to interact within the community and these relationships do not always have to be in depth. Meeting a person for dinner or participating in group activity every so often can be the best medicine!

7. **Find purpose and meaning**. Think about things that bring you joy. Find an outlet for yourself—a place to share your special gifts (Yes! You have gifts). Perhaps volunteering or caregiving brings you fulfillment. Or maybe you enjoy a religious affiliation. Whatever it is, do more of it!

8. **Stay positive**. Surround yourself with positive experiences and people. Take time each day to list things you are grateful for and practice positive thinking.

A healthy outlook and emotional wellness is integral to developing a strong self-esteem. Positive experiences lead to positive thoughts and vice versa. It is a cycle of positivity! Certainly, there will be challenges but you will be prepared to handle those situations with grace if you adopt practices that increase your emotional health. As you master these skills, your self-esteem will soar and you are more likely to feel competent and empowered!

Activity

Scan the QR code, review the list of questions, and mark each statement with a yes, no, or not sure. Identify areas of strength (yes), areas that require additional attention (not sure) and areas that need work (no).

 Scan the QR code to access the emotional health checklist by Lisa Kift, https://loveand life-toolbox.com/hows-your-emotional-health-a-quick-checklist/

How to Ask for Help

Asking for help can be difficult for some people. We are often taught to act independently and care for our own needs without complaint. However, there are times when we may be unable to help ourselves. Perhaps we are too depressed or sad, maybe our energy levels are low or we are physically depleted. In some cases, we may not know what it is that we need exactly. Our insights are blocked and our strength is weakened. You should not be ashamed of any of these circumstances—everyone has those moments. In these instances, it can be difficult to be vulnerable and ask for help but it can be vital to your ongoing health.

Look around you. Are there family and/or friends that you can talk to about your difficulties? If so, this can be a helpful outlet. Let them know that you are having a hard time with life and need someone who will listen. Sometimes just talking about the problems that you are having is a release. If you don't have family members of close friends, there are others who you can count on. Counselors, clergy, and self-help groups are all possibilities. When asking for help—there are no set rules! The important thing is that you do seek assistance when you need it. However, if planning a course of action is important to you, here are a few tips that you may try when asking someone for help.

- Try to find an opportune time when you can have privacy, will not be interrupted and have ample time to share.
- Be transparent and honest. Tell your story as it is, including accurate assessments of how you're feeling. Try to describe your feelings as best you can even if it is difficult.
- Be open regarding what you need (if you know). Ask for what you need, being as specific as you possibly can.
- Be engaged in solution-focused thinking as much as you can; however, if what you mainly need is someone to listen, it is perfectly fine to let them know that you are not necessarily looking for advice—just a friendly ear.
- Follow through—if this person asks you to check in with them regularly to let them know how you are doing—do so! It can help keep you accountable and also help you maintain any gains you may have made.

If you are thinking of harming yourself, please reach out to someone immediately. Your instructor is always here to help! You may also garner an immediate response by calling the National Suicide Prevention Lifeline at 1-800-273-8255.

Resiliency

Image Description: A person climbing a very high rock structure over a lake

Think of a time in your life when you were met with a challenge. Maybe you got cut from a team, your parents got divorced, or you went through a break up. Now think about how you worked through that situation. Maybe you decided to try out for a different team or focused your attention on another hobby. Maybe you sought the support of your friends or a professional when your parents were going through a divorce. Maybe you decided that you would stay single for a while and refocus on yourself and your goals. However, you managed to overcome that adversity, you demonstrated resiliency.

Resilience can be simply defined as bouncing back after a difficult time. More specifically, it is the process of adapting well in the face of adversity, trauma, tragedy, threats, or significant sources of stress. It is a universal capacity. We all have the ability to demonstrate resiliency and when met with challenging or stressful life events, most people are able to adapt successfully over time.

Image Description: A graphic depicting mental resilience that is surrounded by suggestions for increasing resiliency

Ten Ways to Build Resilience

Make connections. Good relationships with close family members, friends, or others are important. Accepting help and support from those who care about you and will listen to you strengthens resilience. Some people find that being active in civic groups, faith-based organizations, or other local groups provides social support and can help with reclaiming hope. Assisting others in their time of need also can benefit the helper.

Avoid seeing crises as insurmountable problems. You can't change the fact that highly stressful events happen, but you can change how you interpret and respond to these events. Try looking beyond the present to how future circumstances may be a little better. Note any subtle ways in which you might already feel somewhat better as you deal with difficult situations.

Accept that change is a part of living. Certain goals may no longer be attainable as a result of adverse situations. Accepting circumstances that cannot be changed can help you focus on circumstances that you can alter.

Move toward your goals. Develop some realistic goals. Do something regularly—even if it seems like a small accomplishment—that enables you to move toward your goals. Instead of focusing on tasks that seem unachievable, ask yourself, "What's one thing I know I can accomplish today that helps me move in the direction I want to go?"

Take decisive actions. Act on adverse situations as much as you can. Take decisive actions, rather than detaching completely from problems and stresses and wishing they would just go away.

Look for opportunities for self-discovery. People often learn something about themselves and may find that they have grown in some respect as a result of their struggle with loss. Many people who have experienced tragedies and hardship have reported better relationships, greater sense of strength even while feeling vulnerable, increased sense of self-worth, a more developed spirituality, and heightened appreciation for life.

Nurture a positive view of yourself. Developing confidence in your ability to solve problems and trusting your instincts helps build resilience.

Keep things in perspective. Even when facing very painful events, try to consider the stressful situation in a broader context and keep a long-term perspective. Avoid blowing the event out of proportion.

Maintain a hopeful outlook. An optimistic outlook enables you to expect that good things will happen in your life. Try visualizing what you want, rather than worrying about what you fear.

Take care of yourself. Pay attention to your own needs and feelings. Engage in activities that you enjoy and find relaxing. Exercise regularly. Taking care of yourself helps to keep your mind and body primed to deal with situations that require resilience.

Additional ways of strengthening resilience may be helpful. For example, some people write about their deepest thoughts and feelings related to trauma or other stressful events in their life. Meditation and spiritual practices help some people build connections and restore hope.

The key is to identify ways that are likely to work well for you as part of your own personal strategy for fostering resilience. Can you think of any other ways to build resilience?

Scan the QR Code to Access the Resiliency Quiz or follow the link: http://www.resiliency.com/free-articles-resources/the-resiliency-quiz/
Please save your results and record them in the next chapter.

End of Chapter Self-Reflection

It's time to reflect on what you have learned about yourself through this chapter. Respond to each open-ended prompt on the staircase and save your answers for the culminating planning session at the end of the course.

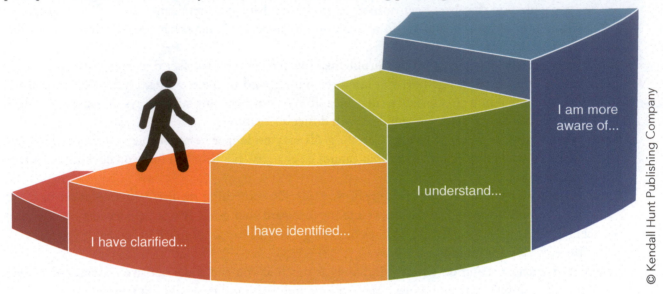

I have clarified...

I have identified...

I understand...

I am more aware of...

References

Beck, Aaron T. (1976). *Cognitive therapies and emotional disorders*. New York: New American Library

Beck, Aaron T. (1972). *Depression; Causes and Treatment*. Philadelphia: University of Pennsylvania Press.

Canadian Mental Health Association BC & Anxiety Canada. (2016). *Wellness module 8: Healthy thinking*. Retrieved from https://www.heretohelp.bc.ca/wellness-module/wellness-module-8-healthy-thinking

FamilyDoctor. Org. (2017). *Mental health: Keeping your emotional health*. Retrieved from https://familydoctor.org/mental-health-keeping-your-emotional-health/

GoodTherapy.org. (2015). *20 cognitive distortions and how they affect your life*. Retrieved from https://www.goodtherapy.org/blog/20-cognitive-distortions-and-how-they-affect-your-life-0407154

Kift, L. (2012). *How's your emotional health: A quick checklist*. Retrieved from https://loveandlifetoolbox.com/hows-your-emotional-health-a-quick-checklist/

CHAPTER 6
Personal Upgrades

Image Description: Photo of an arrow-shaped sign with the words "Next level"

This chapter will help you identify some key strengths and areas of potential growth.

In this chapter, you will:

- Identify your resiliency protective factors
- Think critically about information management
- Better understand the benefits and drawbacks of multitasking
- Assess your relationship with time management

Critical skill development: To invest in recognizing and identifying potential areas of resiliency and strength and potential areas of challenge.

Adapting Successfully to Change

One of the "things" that can get in your way is the inability to adapt to change. Sometimes you get stuck or looped into the same way of thinking and acting. The outcome, of course, is the same old result.

©Ivelin Radkov/shutterstock.com

Image Description: Illustration of a hand drawing a cycle that depicts the words "The same old thinking = the same old results

Sometimes, it takes some whining, crying, yelling at the beginning and sometimes you need to have a pity party to just feel bad about it for a bit. All of that is perfectly okay...as long as you do not get stuck there. So put on your party hat (or lei and sunglasses) and have that pity party....

Then shake it off and make a plan for change!

©Monica Click/shutterstock.com

Image Description: Photo of a dog with pink glasses and a colorful headband on its head

A concept to add to your knowledge base is Cognitive Behavioral Therapy and deal with thought loops that drive behaviors and feelings.

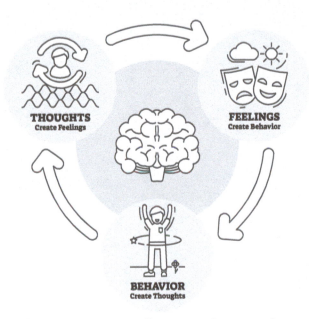

CBT
Cognitive Behavioral Therapy

THOUGHTS
Create Feelings

FEELINGS
Create Behavior

BEHAVIOR
Create Thoughts

©VectorMine/shutterstock.com

Image Description: An illustration depicting the cognitive behavioral therapy process

To improve, impact, or change the thought loop from negative to positive involves interrupting or changing the negative cycle and redirecting it to more positive outcomes. It takes practice to break the old ways and habits of thinking. The challenge is to break out of the same pattern of behavior or reacting to a situation as quickly as possible to move forward to a better way of being.

The first step is to take a look at your Resiliency Protective Factors and see what resources you have to work with for this situation. At this time, if you need to refresh your memory on what constitutes resiliency, please refer back to Chapter 5. The following exercise is suggested to help you get unstuck and move on!

CLEARLY STATE THE SITUATION, FEELING, ISSUE YOU WISH TO CHANGE:

_____

_____

_____

_____

CLEARLY STATE THE SITUATION, FEELING, ISSUE AS IT WOULD BE **AFTER** YOU MAKE THE NECESSARY CHANGES. Include details as how it will feel, how your day might change, how it might impact your health or attitude. Get into the moment of describing how good making this change will impact you. Feel free to draw or doodle in this space as you think freely.

Now you know how good it will be when this change is made—time to make a plan to get there!

©PHOTOCREO Michael Bednarek/
shutterstock.com

Image Description: Illustration of a person standing in the sunset

LIST OF ALL RESILIENCY PROTECTIVE FACTORS (RESULTS FROM RESILIENCY QUIZ AT THE END OF CHAPTER 5) LIST YOUR PROTECTIVE FACTORS IN ORDER OF EFFECTIVENESS WITH NUMBER 1 BEING THE MOST EFFECTIVE.

1.

2.

3.

4.

5.

6.

7.

8.

9.

10.

Circle/highlight the ones that are most critical to adapting to the situation you wish to change.
List all the steps/actions needed to impact this change.

Now, arrange the above steps/actions into the most logical order for implementing.

Step 1.

Step 2.

Step 3.

Step 4.

Step 5.

Step 6.

Step 7.

Step 8.

Step 9.

Step 10. CELEBRATE YOUR SUCCESS!!!

Take a look at your list. Does this look right to you? If not, move them around. For the first three steps, set a target date for addressing and completion. Once those first three steps are completed, evaluate the need for Steps 4 and on. If more action is needed, set target dates for those steps. DO NOT FORGET TO USE YOUR RESILIENCY PROTECTIVE FACTORS~THESE ARE YOUR PERSONAL RESOURCES!!!

Information Management

Our lives are motivated and directed by connection with others. Whether we strive for significant connection with others, a more solitary existence, or somewhere in between—interaction happens. One of the elements of our life satisfaction is this balance in connection—whether by too much, too little or just the right amount. Connection involves communication and communication, or information sharing, in this day and age is constant! In this chapter, we are going to explore information management in a culture where we are constantly bombarded by information via multiple venues and outlets.

One note here: dependent on your age/generation, information dissemination has evolved into different formats.

Image Description: Illustration of two smiley faces

If you are a bit older, you may remember rotary or push button landline telephones and television with no recording options and/or a way to avoid commercials interrupting programming. If you are younger, you may have only known cell phones and internet streaming. It is interesting to note these generational differences. Each year Beloit College publishes "The Mindset List" for the graduating high school class of that year. It is intended to be offered as a list of values that shape the worldview of high school seniors (approximate age of 18). Take a moment to search your list and those of your parents, etc. It is interesting to note the differences and apply that to the upcoming discussions on information management.

Communication in the Digital Age

The ability to communicate via electronics can take some of the risk out of our interactions. For example, some relationships are ended via text. That involves much less skill and angst than standing face to face with someone, looking them in the eye and ending a relationship.

The ability to tap into each other's lives via social media offers another connection that has both positive and negative qualities as well. For some, there is little interest in social media engagement and for some it is an obsession. One term coined from our access to social media is FOMO—the fear of missing out. It's a real thing—take a moment to surf the internet to explore this concept and how it potentially impacts where your energy is going.

Image Description: Photo of a smartphone, notebook, pencil, ear buds, and paper clips with the words "Fear of missing out"

Image Description: Social media

To accommodate this fear, attention to social media posts can become overwhelming and the lives depicted in these posts can be misleading. In one college course, an Instructor asked the students to choose a Facebook, Instagram, or other social media post by an actual friend that they spend time with, not just a social media friend. This post was to depict an event in that friend's life on which they had knowledge. The students were then asked to:

1. Describe the event as seen from the social media post
2. Describe the actual event from the experience of attending the event
3. Determine if the actual event and the social media posted account of the event matched

From this assignment, 90% of the social media posted events did not match the actual life event. One student shared:

The picture posted by my friend shows she and her husband on a beautiful anniversary vacation to Cancun. The water and beach were gorgeous, they are both smiling and look very happy in multiple pictures on their trip. In reality, they were both cheating on each other, so they fought the whole trip and came back to start their divorce. At first, I looked at their vacation picture and was so jealous of their trip together and from this assignment, I realized that this was a fake social media life. They were miserable together and should have just posted a picture of them in one of their frequent screaming

Image Description: Young adults holding up signs with camera, hashtag, headphones

Image Description: People working around a table using technology

matches to be more realistic. It really opened my eyes to the fact that most of the social media lives I envied, were fake. In fact, my life was really happy—in real life, not just for my social media posts. That realization changed my satisfaction with my life and I am glad we had to do this assignment.

The course in which this student was engaged was based on the works of Sherry Turkle and *Reclaiming Conversation in the Digital Age* was one of the base works used in the class. Turkle's works are very powerful and encourage us to look at a healthier use of technology in our communications with each other. More on this topic later, but it is important to note how these information outlets impact our management of information and time.

Outside of the social aspect that 24:7 information outlets provide, there is also global connection and real time news. The ability to tap into the global community and have instant information has its benefits. We, as members of the global community, can see ourselves as such—rather than just the local community that we can physically access. We are more aware and informed than ever before. That is exciting and opens up more possibilities for our lives. The key is healthy use of this constant information stream and self-monitoring so that it does not become an addiction in our lives.

Image Description: A photo of a smartphone and tablet

It can also be anxiety-producing and used to extremes, both of which are unhealthy. As of the writing of this text, in the psychological community, a new diagnosis has been proposed called *Internet Addiction Disorder*. There are some treatment clinics established to treat this new disorder. Additionally, there are new studies studying anxiety in young children that are examining the access to so much information as a potential root cause. Cyber bullying has definitely received massive attention in the media as well. So, "Houston, we could have a problem" with internet overload and information management.

Cyber Safety: How Do You Stay Safe?

Lastly, cyber safety is an area of self-protection that is important for consideration. The following are some quick tips for keeping you and your information safe in the cyber world:

©elenabsl/shutterstock.com

Image Description: Illustration of ways to stay online

The important thing to note about cyber security is that remaining vigilant and up-to-date on trending scams and potential breaches is important. To be a smart and safe user of cyber information, continue to read and review current safety tips on a regular basis. What may be a safe user practice today could get hacked tomorrow. Spend intentional time researching the most up-to-date safe practices to protect your identity!

Image Description: Illustration of blocks that spell out privacy.

During the discussions on wellness, you were tasked with examining the balance of wellness in your life. Apply these same concepts to your current management of 24:7 information flow and to develop healthy usage parameters for yourself. It is also important to apply your skills of critical thinking when synthesizing and analyzing the information in front of you so that you are not "buying in" to everything you read. THINK CRITICALLY AND FOR YOURSELF!

Image Description: Illustration of sign post with two arrows and the words "Fake" and "Real"

The Myth of Multitasking

One last concept to touch upon in this Information Management section is multitasking, or rather **THE MYTH OF MULTITASKING!** Many of us deploy multitasking to keep up with the fast pace of our lives ~ remember *Crazy Busy* discussions in Chapter Three? We may feel that without multitasking, we could not get it all done in a 24-hour day. So, before we begin to look at better planning and time-use strategies, we need to have an honest discussion about the myth of multitasking. For the nay-sayers, some research and information will be shared about multitasking.

Photo Description: Photo of a person looking flustered while trying to multi-task

Research has shown that multitasking is not humanly possible. Before you throw this book down and say that this is not true, take a quick look at the research by the American Psychological Association 2006, which shows:

1. Doing more than one task at a time takes a toll on productivity. Our mind and brain are not designed for heavy duty multitasking and can have catastrophic results for the tasks.
2. Multitasking requires quick switches between tasks. This task juggling has a cost in time for switching between tasks. This time switch cost is impacted by the complexity or familiarity of the tasks involved. "Meyer has said that even brief mental blocks created by shifting between tasks can cost as much as 40 percent of someone's productive time." (https://www.apa.org/research/action/multitask)

So in overprogramming our day to get everything done, we utilize multitasking which might just make the problem bigger. Mental fatigue, frustration, and physical exhaustion can be the result.

That is the bad news. Now here is some good news!

One Vanderbilt University study revealed that multitasking might be improved through training your brain. Your brain needs to be trained to switch between tasks more effectively and efficiently. "Our results imply that the fundamental reason we are lousy multitaskers is because our brains process each task slowly, creating a bottleneck at the central stage of decision making" (Moran, 2009).

Image Description: Photo of a person looking flustered while trying to multi-task

The point of this not to deter you from multitasking, because that is not going to happen. It is to help you better gear your efforts toward maximum productivity. So, let's just see how multitasking works for you by taking a quick test.

Activity

You will need some method of timing yourself (phone, stopwatch, etc.)

Here it is:

1. Identify two activities that you often multitask. If you need suggestions, here is a common multitasking activity pair:
   Texting/responding to social media/answering emails
   Studying/reading a chapter of a textbook

First, clear your area of all distractions. Select a method of timing yourself OR ask someone to time you as you complete the activity. NOTE: If you are timing yourself with the timer on your cellular or other device, you must put the device out of site while completing the task OR you can ask someone to time this activity for you.)

- Enter the time it took to read a chapter of text: _____

- Enter the time it took to check device for emails/texts: _____

Enter the time it took to do the two tasks.

Now, let's multitask.

This time, and again time yourself or have someone time you, read an equivalent chapter of text and keep your devices beside you so that you are free to look at and respond to any texts/snaps/emails/posts that come across your social media.

- Enter the time it took to complete the multiple tasks: _____

The majority of people double the time required to complete the task during round 2 and often a reduction in reading comprehension requiring them to reread the information. During this multitasking round, feelings of frustration and aggravation can also occur. A term called switch-tasking is also applied in activities of this type. Rather than doing more than one task at a time, you are actually doing a quick shift from task to another. The shift can increase the time on task rather than decrease the completion time. More complex tasks make the multitask or switch-task method more difficult.

Consider other instances where you try and multitask and get an honest read for how effective you are in completing these tasks. Time yourself doing each of the tasks individually and compare with the time that it took to multitask. In these situations, be sure you are looking at your accuracy in completing the tasks as well as your stress level in attempting to multitask in determining the success or need for changing your practices. If the goal is to complete more things in less time, maybe multitasking is not working for you. If it is, great! If not, change your game. One challenge to consider is that you may be using multitasking as an avoidance for completing tasks that are unpleasant—just a thought. Work harder not smarter.

To determine your productivity, choose an instance where you typically attempt to multitask. Time yourself doing each of the tasks individually and compare with the time that it took to multitask. In these situations, be sure you are looking at your accuracy in completing the tasks as well as your stress level in attempting to multitask in determining the success or need for change to your practices.

Internet Time Out

There are many multitasking tests just like this one and they are actually fun to do. Take an internet break to check some others out to help you better understand the pros and cons of multitasking.

Time Management

Just as you need to manage the flow of information into and out of your day, it is important to have a grip on time. Managing the use of your time is as important as how you manage your money!

Image Description: Photo of an alarm clock with the words "Time is precious, use it wisely"

Intentionality: Knowing Where My Time Goes and Retooling the Plan

Activity

Image Description: Photo of a person meditating

TIME MANAGEMENT

Steps to Creating a Good Plan

1. Identify where your time goes by creating a time log.
   The time log may be kept in your own day planner or on a daily schedule you create. Keep a time log for one typical week day and typical weekend day.

2. Identify your prime time.
   On the time log created for #1. Highlight those times that are peak or prime times for you as far as energy levels and mental sharpness are concerned.

3. Identify and list problems or "black holes" that take up your time ineffectively or inappropriately.

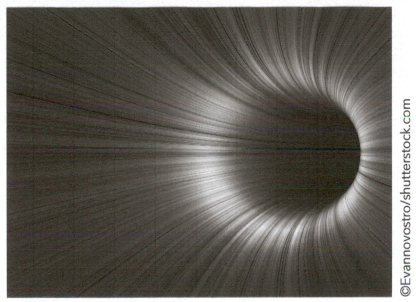

©Evannovostro/shutterstock.com

Image Description: Illustration of a black hole

NOTE: Black holes are not activities that give you a break to recharge or rejuvenate you in some way. For example, if you have hours of homework to do, but you feel guilty that you have taken 30 minutes to go for a walk, have dinner with your family or surf the internet—that is not a black hole. That is much needed down time.

BUT, if you have hours of homework to do and you surf the internet, play video games, or hang out with whomever for 3 hours ~ THAT would be a black hole in your use of time. Those you need to fix!

4. Identify the ways to make these "black holes" disappear and give more intentionality to the use of your time!
5. Revisit the goals you developed in Chapter 2 and apply your new knowledge of how you are planning to better use your time/heartbeats to accomplish your goals.

End of Chapter Self-Reflection

It's time to reflect on what you have learned about yourself through this chapter. Respond to each open-ended prompt on the staircase and save your answers for the culminating planning session at the end of the course.

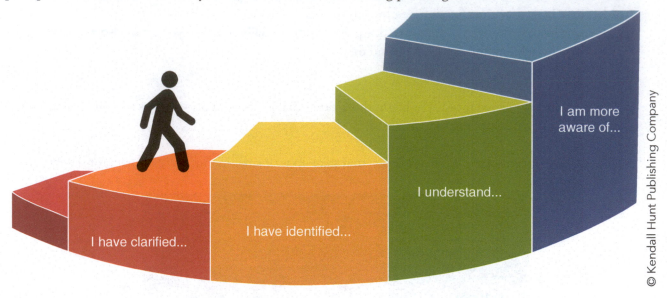

References

American Psychological Association. (2006). Multitasking: Switching costs. Retrieved from https://www.apa.org/research/action/multitask

Moran, M. (2009). Multitasking ability can be improved through training. Retrieved from https://news.vanderbilt.edu/2009/07/15/multitasking-ability-can-be-improved-through-training-84357/

UNIT IV

Relationships and Connections

Image Description: Illustration of two stick figures holding hands

In this unit, you will continue your journey of learning about yourself and others, delving into some new and hopefully challenging topics. You will learn about yourself, your interactions with others, and how to improve both your communication and your relationships with others. Along the way, you will hopefully come to understand how all the components of this course, up to this point (values, decision-making, personality, and goal setting), play a role in healthy relationships. Furthermore, your new awareness of human differences can lead to a better understanding of people from different cultures and backgrounds that most likely have a different way of viewing things than you.

CHAPTER 7
Identifying Important Relationships

Image Description: Photo of many different kinds of people clasping hands

©DisobeyArt/shutterstock.com

This chapter builds on what you have already learned in the first three units, constructing and expanding your awareness beyond yourself and your own styles to learning about others and their ways of doing things. After completing this chapter, you will have learned skills that you need to have healthy relationships and will understand how your values are at the core of these important topics. You will examine your personal self-esteem, where it comes from, how to build it, and how it affects all your relationships and interactions.

In this chapter, you will

- Explore your relationship with yourself, learning how to develop greater self-respect
- Gain an understanding of your family of origin dynamics and rules and how they have shaped you and continue to influence you
- Learn about the components necessary for a healthy relationship including interacting with others effectively, fighting fair, and ending relationships in a constructive way

Critical Skill Development: To identify and examine important relationships in your life.

Relationships and Systems

Have you ever heard the saying, "It takes a village to raise a child"? This comes from an African proverb, which highlights the importance of how community influences the growth and development of a child. The idea that the village or community is an important factor in our environment does not end in childhood. We never exist in isolation, therefore our relationships and communities are always an important factor to consider. In this section, you will learn about the importance of relationships and will take time to identify and examine key relationships in your life.

First, let's take a moment to understand why relationships are so important. From the time we are children, our environment and the people within that environment play an important role in our experiences and development. Bronfenbrenner (1979) developed an ecological model that involved nested systems that interact and influence an individual's environment. The model includes bi-directional influences, which indicate that the interactions are not one direction but rather the individual can also affect the environment and people within the system. The ecological model is made up of five distinct but interactive layers including the microsystem, mesosystem, exosystem, macrosystem, and chronosystem.

Sincero, S. M. (2012, March 14). Ecological systems theory. Retrieved from https://explorable.com/ecological-systems-theory

Image Description: Photo of three children playing with puzzle pieces.

1. The Micro System

The micro system's setting is the direct environment we have in our lives. Your family, friends, classmates, teachers, neighbors, and other people who have a direct contact with you are included in your micro system. The micro system is the setting in which we have direct social interactions with these social agents. The theory states that we are not mere recipients of the experiences we have when socializing with these people in the micro system environment, but we are contributing to the construction of such an environment.

2. The Mesosystem

The mesosytem involves the relationships between the microsystems in one's life. This means that your family experience may be related to your school experience. For example, if a child is neglected by his parents, he may have a low chance of developing positive attitude toward his teachers. Also, this child may feel awkward in the presence of peers and may resort to withdrawal from a group of classmates.

3. The Exosystem

The exosystem is the setting in which there is a link between the context in which the person does not have any active role, and the context in which the person actively participates. Suppose a child is more attached to his father than his mother. If the father goes abroad to work for several months, there may be a conflict between the mother and the child's social relationship, or on the other hand, this event may result in a tighter bond between the mother and the child.

4. The Macrosystem

The macrosystem setting is the actual culture of an individual. The cultural contexts involve the socioeconomic status of the person and/or his family, his ethnicity, or race and living in a still developing or a Third World country. For example, being born to a poor family makes a person work harder every day.

5. The Chronosystem

The chronosystem includes the transitions and shifts in one's lifespan. This may also involve the socio-historical contexts that may influence a person. One classic example of this is how divorce, as a major life transition, may affect not only the couple's relationship but also their children's behavior. According to a majority of research, children are negatively affected on the first year after the divorce. The next years after it would reveal that the interaction within the family becomes more stable and agreeable.

Relationship with Self

The most important relationship in your life is with yourself. In order to successfully navigate all relationships in the best possible way, it is important that you have a strong sense of self. How often do you spend time alone? Is intentional personal growth and self-reflection important to you? Why or why not? Taking a good look at ourselves can be intimidating, challenging, and even a bit scary but it can also be extremely rewarding and can help us create a more clear picture of who we want to be and what we want out of life.

In chapter one, you were able to identify your core values. Now it is time to go one step further and think about how well you know yourself beyond identification of your values. Here, you will start to explore knowing yourself fully and deeply. Knowing what matters to you the most, what you're passionate about, and what you want out of life. The following questions are not meant to be easy. In fact, you may not be able to answer them all right now. There are no right or wrong answers. There is only you uncovering the process of building a closer relationship with the person within.

Activity: Self-reflection

1. What activities in your life bring you joy?

2. What is something you always love doing? What about it do you love?

3. What do you fear about leaving something or someone behind, even if it does not bring value or joy to your life?

4. List three to five things that you have accomplished in your life that you are most proud of.

5. Describe the way you want people to perceive you. What impact do you want to leave?

6. How are you making a difference in the world? Your local community?

7. If you could have one single wish granted, what would it be?

8. In the haste of your daily life, what are you not seeing?

9. Describe your most important core value. How did this value become the most important to you?

10. Describe how you evaluate or get to know others when you first meet them.

11. How confident are you in your abilities to make important decisions? Elaborate.

12. What is your greatest limitation that you place on yourself?

13. Who is the most important person in your life?

14. Describe your most influential role model.

15. Who is a person that you don't enjoy spending time with but still do? Why?

16. What is a truth or mantra you live by?

17. Describe your moral compass.

18. Describe a "failure" that you have turned into a life lesson.

19. Describe what role gratitude plays in your life.

20. What are you most grateful for?

21. Describe your relationship with money and material possessions.

22. If you were forced to eliminate every physical possession from your life with the exception of what could fit into a single backpack, what would you put in it?

23. How do you feel about getting older?

24. What makes you most uncomfortable? Do you avoid being uncomfortable or embrace it?

25. At this point in time, what do you believe is the meaning of your life?

Finding Your Tribe

Now we are going to shift the focus to identifying and evaluating the key relationships in your life. A "tribe" is a human social group that often has some common threads. Many times, people come and go from our lives and we aren't intentional about honoring what those relationships bring when they come into our lives or take away when they leave. It is always a healthy practice to reevaluate the relationships in your life and make sure you are surrounded by people who augment your life and are aligned with your values. This does not mean that you always have to agree or that you can't have friends whose values and beliefs are different from your own. In fact, having people in your life who are diverse in many ways can enhance your

Image Description: Photo of six people standing close together with arms behind each other's backs

©Rawpixel.com/shutterstock.com

life experience and contribute to personal growth. Instead, it is important that you evaluate that you aren't sacrificing your values to remain in a relationship that is unhealthy. Finding your tribe is about finding and surrounding yourself with a community of people who make you feel valued. It is also important to note that this community should love and accept you 100% for who you are, as you are. These are people who just seem to "get" you. You should not have to alter your appearance, dress, personality, or anything else to feel like part of your tribe. Your true tribe will accept you unconditionally as your most authentic self.

Our tribe are those individuals who make up our inner circle. We are likely to spend a lot of time with these individuals and share our thoughts, feelings, and experiences more freely. In other words, these are the relationships in our lives with the greatest levels of intimacy, vulnerability, and trust.

What are some of the most important qualities that you value in your interpersonal relationships? Do you value the quality of relationships or quantity? A very good start to relationship proactivity is to map all the people who are present in your life, which we will do in the following activity.

Activity: Relationships

Step 1: Examine your interpersonal relationships by making two lists. In the first list, describe all your relationships that are more personal. The second list should describe all the relationships that are more impersonal. Are you satisfied with the number of quality interpersonal relationships you have identified?

Step 2: Now, read through the lists and place each person on your circle in the appropriate location according to the following definitions:

Intimacy—Include those who you can't imagine your life without. You probably spend a lot of time with these individuals and share a great deal of your personal self with them. You share intimacy and vulnerability with them (does not have to be romantic).

Influence—Includes people you are close to and interact with on a regular basis but with whom you do not share as much intimacy or depth. You likely share some personal information with them but may choose not to share quite as much as you would with someone in your intimate circle. You may share a common bond or history with these individuals.

Affiliation—Includes people you may interact with frequently and you know them fairly well. You have a familiarity and comfort with them but your communication does not include much personal information or depth.

Acquaintance—This circle often includes co-workers, people you know from your community, and acquaintances. You may cross paths with these individuals from time to time but when you do, you may acknowledge them without striking up a conversation. If you do have conversation, it would likely be basic and surface level.

Beyond the circle—Includes people who we know and have interactions with but do not include in our circles. Examples might include your doctor, hairdresser, or other individuals with whom you interact in only a transactional type of way.

Step 3: Draw an arrow to each person. Indicate if you want to move them more inward (build a closer relationship) or if you want to create more distance, maybe even cutting them off completely.

Key Points:

- People don't always have someone in every circle, all the time.
- Different behavior is appropriate in different circles.
- People can shift—in either direction.
- Typically, no one moves from an outer circle to an inner circle immediately.
- No one may come into your inner circle unless you want them to be there.
- You cannot enter someone else's inner circles unless they wish you to.

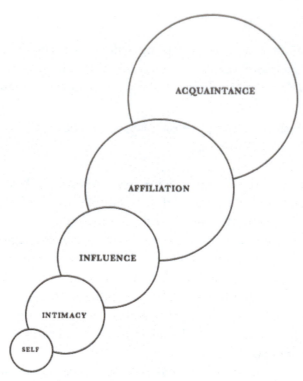

Image Description: Circles with the words self,
intimacy, influence, affiliation, and acquaintance.
Source: Bethany Novotny

Bonus Activity

Take this exercise a step further by using a new diagram. In the second diagram, you can **zoom into the intimate relationship circle** and analyze who are really the closest to you in your life.

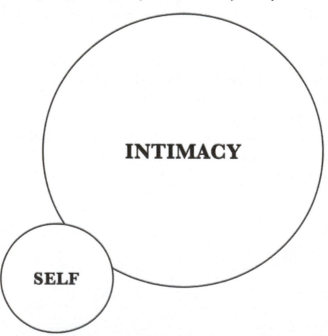

Image Description: Small circle with the word self and
large circle with the word intimacy.
Source: Bethany Novotny

Healthy Relationships

Relationships are an essential part of our everyday lives as human beings. We need relationships to be healthy, and when our relationships are healthy themselves, it adds to our life enjoyment and satisfaction. From the time you were born until this very moment, you have been in relationships with others, and those relationships have helped sustain, support, nurture, encourage, challenge, and develop you into the person you are now. Some may have been more harmful than others, some were likely essential to your survival, and all of them have added to your life in ways that you may not even be aware of.

Image Description: Photo of dog and cat cuddling

©Okeanas/shutterstock.com

Relationships present themselves in our lives in many forms. From acquaintances, friends, co-workers and family, to romantic partners, they all are important in the process of our own growth and in our perception of ourselves. When you think about the most important elements of a healthy relationship, what kinds of things come to mind? Where did you learn what makes a healthy relationship? It is likely that you may have learned some of what you know about relationships (whether healthy or not) from your parents, significant others in the past or present, peers, and one of the biggest sources, media.

While there are many types and structures of relationships, most of the topics in this lesson will be in the context of romantic relationships, but always keep in mind that this applies also to friendships, work relationships, and familial relationships.

> *"The greatest source of happiness for humans comes from our positive relationships. Perhaps the greatest source of human distress also comes from our relationships."*

So, what is it that attracts you to someone in the first place?

- Initial attraction is based upon physical and personality characteristics
- The primary attraction for long-term relationships is comfort based upon familiarity; you tend to be attracted to characteristics, both good and bad, that you are already familiar with as a result of being around your family members

What is compatibility really based on?

- Family rules
- Personality dynamics
- Interests
- Values (ultimately the most important determinant)

Where do we get our dynamics for relationships?

- Your initial relationship pattern is based upon your parental one
- Raising awareness of family of origin dynamics and rules helps you understand your own patterns in relationships and your views on interactions in those relationships
- Once you have identified areas you'd like to change after raising awareness of your family of origin dynamics, you can develop a new model based on healthier dynamics
- This requires dealing with discomfort and finding a new sense of familiarity

There are two basic requirements for a healthy relationship that *must* be present in order for the relationship to be beneficial to all parties, minimizing the harm to any of the members—**Respect** and **Assertiveness**.

Consider why you think these two qualities are the most important components for a relationship as opposed to such aspects as love, honesty, trust, etc. Write down your own definition of each of the terms above in regard to why they are so important in relationships:

Respect: _____
Assertiveness: _____

While respect and assertiveness are the two basic requirements for a healthy relationship, there are, of course, others that are important in a relationship. Here is a model that may help you understand the five main dimensions of healthy relationships:

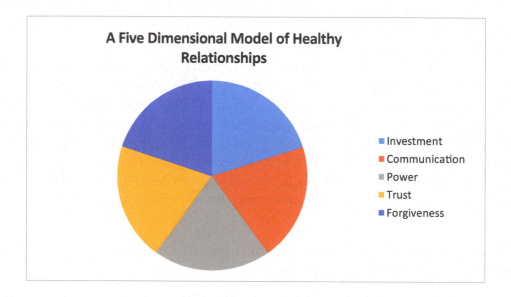

Investment means: doing everything you can possibly do to enhance your partner's life experience
Communication means:

- Developing rules for your process of problem solving
- Making it a priority to sit down regularly to discuss issues and plans
- Giving your relationship time to talk with each other
- Respect, respect, and more respect
- Taking timeouts when necessary
- Practicing reflective listening

Power is:

- The shift from taking care of oneself to taking care of the relationship
- The balance of power that serves the relationship best
- Based upon personal strengths and differences in personality
- The area that tends to reflect the greatest abuses

Trust is:

- The barometer of the relationship
- Essential to the healthy functioning of any relationship; to lack trust in a relationship is simply counterproductive
- Essential to having clean communication and balanced power

Forgiveness is:

- Essential to maintain long-term relationships
- Helps couple focus on present needs
- The process of letting go of baggage and hurtful memories
- Can take its own time to emerge

You've seen that respect is already included in the communication dimension of this healthy relationship model and is essential for each of the other components as well. Respect is a core piece of relationships because without it, there is little to build on. If you truly respect someone, you care enough to invest. Respect requires that you learn about the other and in doing so you are also empowered to treat them the way they would like to be treated. Respect is essential to all good relationships as is assertiveness. We will discuss assertiveness more in depth toward the end of the chapter.

What is your Language of Love?

Another aspect of exploring healthy relationships is knowing how you give and receive love. The idea that the "right person" will just come along and know immediately the best way to love you; that they will be able to just meet your emotional needs without you ever voicing them is highly unlikely. Instead, great relationships happen because people communicate clearly and directly. They are willing to be vulnerable with one another. They happen because they are willing to teach each other where their boundaries are and how they prefer to be loved.

Love Language of **Touch**   Love Language of **Service**   Love Language of **Words**   Love Language of **Time**   Love Language of **Gift**

©kristnu/shutterstock.com

Image Description: Five Love Languages.

Activity: Love Languages

Interested in finding out your Love Language? Scan the QR code to take the quiz now!

Go to http://www.5lovelanguages.com/profile/

©TairA/shutterstock.com

Image Description: Picture of a multi-colored hand giving the sign for "love" in ASL.

When it asks whether you are married or single, click single. (Click single even if you're married/partnered.) The questionnaire for singles is better-designed and worded than the questionnaire for those who are married or in a relationship.

Fill out the 30-item questionnaire to respond to the following questions:

1. What is your primary love language?

2. Do you have a strong love-language preference (i.e., is it clear that you have one preferred love language, or do you score almost equally across two or more love languages)?

3. If you took the love languages questionnaire, do you agree with the results?

4. When are the times that you have felt well-loved by your partner or others (in person *and* at a distance)?

5. List five ways you would like your partner to show you love through your primary love language.

If you are partnered:

6. What is your partner's primary love language(s)?

7. If you and your partner have different love languages, what sorts of misunderstandings, hurt feelings, or conflict might arise from these different preferences?

8. List five ways you could show your partner you care for them by speaking a love language that's important to them.

ACTIVITY: COMPATIBILITY

Since we've been talking so much about relationships, what goes into them, and how to maintain them, you now get a chance to see what kind of people with whom you are compatible. You may already have an idea, but most students tend to be surprised after doing this activity to find that they are compatible with more people than they realized.

In this exercise find someone or a group of people with whom you can discuss the following questions. If you are doing this with a group, you can compare this to speed-dating and provide a reasonable time for each dyad to communicate before changing partners.

1. Are you independent?
2. What are your values?

   3. How do you think kids should be raised?
   4. What kind of interests (hobbies) do you have?
   5. How did you grow up?
   6. How did the people who raised you get along?
   7. What are your goals in life?
   8. Expectations of relationships?
   9. What do you believe in? (whatever you take this to mean)
   10. Are you religious or spiritual?
   11. Who do you admire and why?
   12. Do you feel you are responsible? (support your answer)
   13. How did your last relationship go?
   14. What are your political beliefs?
   15. How open are you to new things and experiences?
   16. Do you have a sense of humor and how does it work?
   17. How is your hygiene?
   18. Do you have children? Ex-spouses?
   19. How do you define your sexuality?
   20. What are your boundaries regarding cheating in relationships?
   21. Who do you turn to when you are stressed by your relationship?

To wrap up our section on healthy relationships, we have included a table that compares healthy relationships with unhealthy ones. This is a chance for you to see all the topics we've covered on relationships in a "big picture" kind of way.

Healthy vs. Unhealthy Relationships

People in healthy relationships respect each other. They can talk honestly and freely to each other and share power and control over decisions. They trust and support each other and respect each other's independence. In contrast, an *unhealthy relationship* is unbalanced. One partner (a person in the relationship) tries to control the other.

Healthy Relationships vs. Unhealthy Relationships

HEALTHY RELATIONSHIPS vs UNHEALTHY RELATIONSHIPS
Equality vs Control—In a healthy relationship, you should make decisions together and respect one another's thoughts and feelings.
Honesty vs Dishonesty—In a healthy relationship, there should be trust and both partners should be truthful, even when it's hard.
Physical safety vs Abuse—In a healthy relationship, you should never feel threatened or mistreated by you partner physically, mentally, or emotionally.
Respect vs Disrespect—In a healthy relationship, you should feel valued and feel like you matter.
Comfort vs Intimidation—In a healthy relationship, you should feel like you can talk to your partner. You should never feel like you must sacrifice your family, friends, or yourself to keep your partner happy.
Sexual respectfulness vs Abuse—In a healthy relationship, you should never feel pressured or forced to participate in any sexual activity that you do not desire. You always have the right to say no.
Independence vs Dependence—In a healthy relationship, both partners can maintain their differentiated identity. In an unhealthy relationship, the partners may become enmeshed and have difficulty maintaining their independence.
Humor vs Hostility—In a healthy relationship, both partners genuinely enjoy spending time together and maintain a "lightness" in their relationship. In an unhealthy relationship, one might feel belittled or like they must walk on eggshells to maintain the peace.

Communication

As humans, we are in constant communication with one another. Even when you are alone in your room studying and your roommate is downstairs watching TV, you are communicating "I need to focus on studying at this moment, and watching TV with you does not allow me to get much studying done." However, your roommate may get the message, "I would rather sit in my room alone with my textbooks than watch TV with you." It is obvious that you cannot control anyone else or the way they receive your communication, whether it passes with words or not. What you *can* control is the *way* in which you communicate. We each have a personal responsibility to communicate in a respectful, effective way, and although this doesn't always happen, below are some guidelines to follow that will help you when you are having difficulty communicating. These can be used in any relationship, no matter the depth or emotional involvement. Anytime you want to address something that is difficult or could be potentially hurtful, consider the following "commandments:"

THE 10 COMMANDMENTS OF CLEAN COMMUNICATION

Adapted from *Couple Skills: Making your relationship work (McKay, Panning, & Paleg, 2006).*

1. <u>Avoid judgmental words and loaded terms.</u>
   This relates to using terms that convey to your partner that he/she is flawed. Words that attack or undermine your partner's feelings of worth have no place in a caring relationship.

2. <u>Avoid global labels.</u>
   This relates to general condemnation of your partner. Such terms as stupid, sexist, crazy, selfish, etc. fall into this category. The outcome of using such words is a loss of trust and closeness.

3. <u>Avoid "you" messages of blame and accusation.</u>
   The essence of the you message is that, "I'm in pain and you did it to me." The message also reflects that, "you were bad and wrong for doing it to me." Use *I messages* that reflect ownership of your feelings instead.

4. <u>Avoid old history.</u>
   Good communication is succinct and focused. It sticks with the current issue and is specific. References to old history are often just building a case as to how bad your partner really is. It uses past transgressions to establish support for how bad your partner is and has no place in a good relationship.

5. <u>Avoid negative comparisons.</u>
   Negative comparisons only punish and put down your partner. A primary goal for a good relationship is to enhance your partner's self-esteem.

6. <u>Avoid threats.</u>
   The basic message of a threat is that you are or will be bad, and I will punish you if you are. Taking a position where you will inflict pain and/or suffering upon your partner is simply counterproductive.

7. <u>Describe your feelings rather than attack with them.</u>
   Describing your feelings provide clarification and promote enhanced understanding. Having a mutual understanding that feelings will be listened to and respected can contribute to a positive relationship. In stating your feelings, it is helpful to keep your voice to a normal volume and inflection.

8. <u>Keep your body language open and receptive.</u>
   Be aware that non-verbal communication is stronger than verbal. If you want your partner to listen or feel that you are listening it is important to maintain good eye contact, to use non-verbal cue's to confirm that you are listening, to keep your body posture open, to model attentiveness, and to keep your face loose and relaxed.

9. <u>Use whole messages.</u>

Whole messages consist of observations, thoughts, feelings, and needs or wants. Observations are statements of facts that are neutral, without judgment, or interference. Thoughts are your beliefs, opinions, theories, and interpretations. Feelings are often the most important and simply describe the emotional state. Needs simply express what you want.

10. <u>Use clear messages.</u>
    Clear messages separate observations, opinions, feelings, and needs. Communicating observations, opinions, feelings, and needs congruently bring consistency to your message and enhance your partner's understanding.

Here are some other helpful guidelines for positive communication:

- Express negative messages through words, but positive messages through both verbal and non-verbal channels.
- Focus upon each other with no distraction as working on something communicates the low value of the other's message.
- Allow time for each other to communicate and time to just be together. Providing such time demonstrates that you consider each other a priority. People also need time to be alone.
- Uncensored, open communication may be more than your relationship can handle. Be sensitive to other's touchy areas and approach them tactfully when you must. Timing can be critical.
- Avoid quarrelling over things that would have been better left unsaid. There are things about all of us that are difficult or even impossible to change. Acceptance may be far more productive than confrontation.
- People tend to weigh negative aspects of communication more heavily than the positive ones. Build positives if you really want the other person to hear you in a constructive way instead of just turning you off.
- Too many positive messages may reduce the level of social interaction.
- Nonverbal communication is generally more powerful than verbal.
- Explicit negative communications may be honest, but may be more destructive than helpful.
- Communication is a process of negotiation. Be attentive to bids and counterbids.

Implementing all these "commandments" and "guidelines" doesn't mean that changing the way you communicate is going to be as "easy as 1, 2, 3." In its most basic form, changing the way you communicate looks like this:

FIVE STEPS TO COMMUNICATION CHANGE

- Listen.
- Use measured self-expression.
- Be selective at making requests.
- Provide positive and corrective feedback.
- Clarify communication so that the intended meaning is arrived at.

More than likely, you have communicated with a wide range of people in your lifetime. Some have been easy to talk to—you felt heard, understood, and respected—while others have been rude, selfish, and always thinking of what they will say next instead of focusing on what you are saying (or maybe you are guilty of those things yourself). Either way, we usually have no problem identifying those we can go to talk to, and those who are better with less serious conversations. To give you an idea, here are some characteristics of both good and bad listeners:

A Good Listener...

- Separates their emotions from other's words.
- Is fully committed to listening to others.

- Waits for the other to complete the message before expressing their own ideas.
- Uses analytic skills to supplement listening.

A Bad Listener...

- Rejects words from others as they are uninteresting, already known, too simple, or too complicated.
- Attends to the speaker's appearance and manner instead of to their spoken message.
- Stops attentively listening to the whole message and concentrates on a key word or phrase.
- Predicts what they will hear and fails to hear the real message.
- What kind of listener are you? Did reading these characteristics bring up anything in your personal life that is a good example of either?

It is clear at this point that no relationship can survive without healthy communication. You have probably heard friends or family members say "He just doesn't listen to anything I say!" or, "She never listens to my side of the story, always assuming she knows what I'm going to say!" Many couples decide to go to couples counseling with their main goal for therapy being "We just need to learn to communicate." Communication also builds or breaks down friendships, family relationships, and work relationships. Adhering to clean communication is a way of respecting others, which is why when it is not practiced you tend to find discord in relationships.

A big part of clean and healthy communication is having the knowledge and awareness of its importance and how to implement it. Once you have that you can foster healthy relationships with minimal conflict. The sad reality is that conflict exists in every relationship in some form or another.

It is also important to note that we have the power to use clean and healthy communication even when others don't. Continuing to not raise your voice during an argument will encourage the other person not to raise their voice. It is essential to know how you communicate and below is a quick assessment to identify your communication style.

Interpersonal Relationships—Vulnerability and Assertiveness

Assertiveness is your ability to act in harmony with your self-esteem, without hurting others.

©VectorMine/shutterstock.com

Image Description: Illustration of a person sitting next to a large heart with an unopened lock

Vulnerability

In the picture above we see a heart that has been bruised and injured. Yet, the heart remains unlocked and open. The figure at the left is reaching upward to release hearts into the sky and presumably spread love and joy. What does this picture tell us about vulnerability and assertiveness? Perhaps it indicates that even though we sometimes find our heart battered, we do well to remain open to others and return positivity to the world in response. Or maybe it says something about the human experience of living and loving—that it can be both painful and joyful but that the outcome all depends on how we interpret the things that happen to us. What do you think?

Being *open* to new experiences and people is often touted as healthy. According to society, we should embrace these novel experiences with gusto! However, being *vulnerable* sounds like a completely different story. When you think of the word "vulnerable", how do you feel? Is vulnerability more often looked at as positive or negative? When something or someone is vulnerable, we tend to think of them as defenseless, weak, and susceptible. It can seem scary to be vulnerable! We tend to want to protect ourselves so that we are not hurt—that is a natural human reaction. Yet, what happens when we become so distracted by avoiding discomfort that we lose out on many experiences or avoid opportunities?

Vulnerability does not have to be a bad thing. In fact, being vulnerable can open up a whole new set of experiences for you. With vulnerability, relationships can mature and deepen, we can embrace novel and new experiences that we never had before (and very well may love them!), and we stretch our capacity for joy and life immersion. When your defenses are always up, you can miss out! Relationships can only go so far, your desire to experience new things can be thwarted and your sense of self could be compromised. Being vulnerable does not necessarily equate to pain. Instead it opens up life's possibilities and enables you to have a broader and deeper capacity to enjoy and experience life.

The secret is balance. If we learn to balance our ability to be vulnerable and open with a skill set that enables us to also be assertive, then we can be better prepared to meet life head on. Being vulnerable does not have to mean that you are a push over or someone who is easily taken advantage of and one way to ensure that is to become adept at using *assertive communication*.

Image Description: Photo of a person holding a duckling in their hand

©BlackOnyx7/shutterstock.com

©Anton Shaparenko/shutterstock.com

Image Description: Illustration of a person pushing a gear with the word "Assertiveness"

We are all familiar with the importance of effective communication in our professional and daily lives. Good communication skills often require practice though and as we age, the ways that we choose to communicate can change; however, most people have a "go-to" way of communicating with others—a style they feel most comfortable with and one that they use most often. Four of the ways in which you might communicate are passively, assertively, passively aggressive and aggressively. Let's explore each type.

Passive Communication

People who communicate passively often defer to others and do not exert their needs or preferences. They prefer to let others express themselves and "go with the flow." Because the passive communicator often ignores their own needs, resentment and anger can easily build. Many times, good ideas are not shared because the passive person does not want to impose their viewpoints on others. Sometimes passive communicators can exhibit physical traits of passivity as well—slumped shoulders, poor eye contact, and diminutive body posture. While there are some situations when passive communicators can be easy to work with—such as working out a consensus or solving a complex problem, often their voices are unnecessarily subdued and silenced. Examples of phrases that passive communicators often use are "whatever you want" or "it doesn't matter to me."

Aggressive Communication

Aggressive communication is often easy to spot. Aggressive communicators are typically, loud, unreasonable, and intimidating. They are forceful about their opinions and often only take their own needs into consideration. They use criticizing, threatening, or demeaning tactics to dominate the conversation, even becoming extremely abusive at times. Examples of phrases that aggressive communicators often use are "I will get my way", "I am right and you are wrong", and "it's all your fault."

Passive-Aggressive Communication

According to the article, 4 Types of Communication Styles (2018), "Passive-aggressive communication style users appear passive on the surface, but within he or she may feel powerless or stuck, building up a resentment that leads to seething or acting out in subtle, indirect or secret ways."

"Most passive-aggressive communicators will mutter to themselves rather than confront a person or issue. They have difficulty acknowledging their anger, use facial expressions that don't correlate with how they feel and even deny there is a problem" (4 Types of Communication Styles, 2018).

"Passive-aggressive communicators are most likely to communicate with body language or a lack of open communication to another person, such as giving someone the silent treatment, spreading rumors behind people's backs or sabotaging others' efforts. Passive-aggressive communicators may also appear cooperative but may silently be doing the opposite. Ultimately, passive-aggressive communicators are aware of their needs,

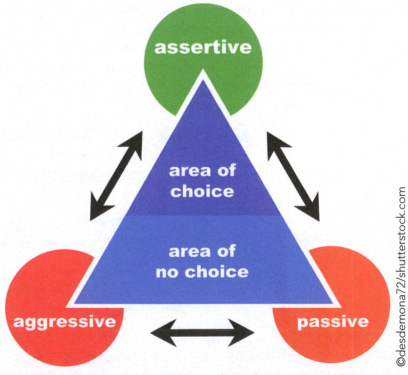

©desdemona72/shutterstock.com

FIGURE 3 Assertive, aggressive, and passive communication

but at times struggle to voice them." (4 Types of Communication Styles, 2018). Examples of phrases that those with passive-aggressive communication style may use are, "that's fine with me but don't get surprised if someone else gets mad" and "that's a really great idea" (said sarcastically).

Figure 3 illustrates the area of entrapment that one can find themselves in when using aggressive, passive, or passive-aggressive communication. When you communicate in one of those ways, you leave the person that you are talking to with few choices. Collaboration and consensus building are shut down. There is no room to compromise or discuss. However, when you use assertive communication, you leave room for choices—both for you and for the person or persons you are speaking with. Assertiveness allows you to express your feelings and thoughts in a constructive way, while leaving the floor open for others to do the same.

Assertive Communication

According to the Impact Factory (2019), a communication training entity, assertive communication is defined as a manner of communicating information (positive or negative) in an open, honest and transparent way. It recognizes the rights of both the speaker and those that are being spoken to. Assertive communication provides opportunities for consensus building and freedom of choice. It is direct but respectful.

©enterlinedesign/shutterstock.com

Image Description: Photo of the word "Voice" on a painted piece of wood

Some advantages of assertiveness skills in communication according to the Impact Factory (2019)

- "Assertiveness helps us feel good about ourselves and others
- Assertiveness leads to the development of mutual respect with others
- Assertiveness increases our self-esteem
- Assertiveness helps us achieve our goals
- Assertiveness minimizes hurting and alienating other people
- Assertiveness reduces anxiety
- Assertiveness protects us from being taken advantage of by others
- Assertiveness enables us to make decisions and free choices in life
- Assertiveness enables us to express, both verbally and non-verbally, a wide range of feelings and thoughts, both positive and negative"

When you tend to speak or act passively, being assertive can almost feel aggressive! However, letting your needs, expectations, and limitations be known is healthy, not aggressive. Assertive communication allows you to take responsibility for yourself and does not promote blaming others. AND it can still be polite and gracious. *How* you say things is as important as what you say. So please don't mistake assertiveness for being rude!

Characteristics of assertiveness in communication

According to the Impact Factory (2019), the following are indicators of assertive communication

- "good eye contact: demonstrates interest, shows sincerity
- body posture: congruent body language will improve the significance of the message
- gestures: appropriate gestures help to add emphasis
- voice: a level, modulated tone is more convincing and acceptable, and is not intimidating
- timing: use your judgment to maximize receptivity and impact
- content: how, where, and when you choose to comment is probably more important than WHAT you say"

The Importance of Using "I" Statements

When you use "I" statements, you are taking responsibility for your own feelings, thoughts, and actions. These statements put you at the center of the equation. Here are a few examples of I statements.

- I feel frustrated when you leave your dirty clothes on the floor. I don't like to have to carry them to the laundry room.
- I find it confusing when you give me a low grade on my assignment but do not offer feedback as to why.
- I wish I could say "yes" to your request but I need to say "no" at this time.

Techniques for building assertive communication skills according to the Impact Factory (2019)

- Rehearse what you want to say and how you want to present yourself. Practice your "I" statements and look in the mirror to gauge your body language. Rehearsing can help you divorce the statements that you wish to make from strong emotions.
- Repeat yourself as much as is needed during the conversation. Stick to your point even when confronted with manipulation or coercion.
- Fogging: This practice helps you to acknowledge criticism without becoming defensive or overly apologetic. In this case, there may be some degree of truthfulness to what is being said—acknowledge that but remain in control of your own choices and actions.
- Negative inquiry/assertion: occurs when you actively seek out constructive criticism from others by prompting the expression of honest feelings to improve communication. Listen to critical comments, acknowledge them, and then use that information to further your understanding of the other person. There is no need to apologize but do acknowledge if you have some responsibility in what the other person has said.

Image Description: A person's hand pointing to the words "Assert yourself"

©Vintage Tone/shutterstock.com.

■ Workable compromise: when and if you feel that your self-respect is not in question, consider a compromise. However, if the end product involves compromising your self-worth or self-respect, return to your original point and reassert yourself.

Although there are no guarantees that assertive communication will always get you what you want, it does dramatically increase the chances that your needs will be voiced and that you will leave the conversation with a sense of self. Most people will appreciate your desire to be direct and straightforward, even if they disagree with your conjecture. Striking a balance between assertiveness and vulnerability can be challenging but with practice and an increased awareness of your needs, you can be both!

Boundaries

"Having healthy boundaries is a form of self-love and self-respect."
LaWhimsy/Monday Mantra

In this chapter we have discussed healthy relationships, effective communication and assertiveness. Now let's turn our attention to the topic of boundaries. Perhaps more than any other aspect of relationships, developing and maintaining healthy boundaries can be challenging. Often, when we care for someone, we want to do whatever is possible to make them happy or demonstrate our affection—and this can be a wonderful experience! Giving in relationships can be just as rewarding as receiving. However, when find that we are extending ourselves beyond healthy limits, we can grow stressed, resentful, and overwhelmed. These feelings can

©GoodStudio/shutterstock.com

Image Description: An illustration of a person sitting in a bubble while several other people try to force their way in

negatively affect the relationship that we cherish, resulting in tension and even anger.

To protect important relationships (as well *the* most important relationship—the one we have with ourselves), it is imperative that we practice developing and maintaining healthy boundaries. This is certainly easier said than done! But once you become increasingly aware of your own needs and feelings, recognizing the necessity of setting healthy boundaries will be easier!

What is a boundary?

"Personal **boundaries** are the physical, emotional, and mental limits we establish to protect ourselves from being manipulated, used, or violated by others. They allow us to separate who we are, and what we think and feel, from the thoughts and feelings of others" (Hereford, 2019). Boundaries are the framework from which we build healthy relationships.

Healthy Boundaries

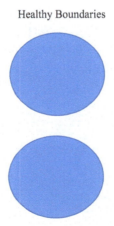

Unhealthy Boundaries

When we set boundaries with others, we are not being mean to them—no! We are being respectful of ourselves. Unhealthy boundaries lead to a break down in relationships. Let's see what unhealthy boundaries may look like.

According to the website, Habits for Wellbeing (2019), unhealthy boundaries may include the following:

- Oversharing—telling everything that you know
- Becoming overly familiar with someone when you first meet them
- Quickly and indiscriminately falling in love
- Not noticing when someone else's boundaries are unhealthy
- Over or under eating
- Letting others have control over your life
- Letting another person define what you believe in
- Going against your own personal values and beliefs to "keep the peace"
- Not noticing when others are invading your space
- Accepting something that you really don't want to—food, gifts, touch
- Touching another person without asking
- Overgiving to the point of unhealthy self-sacrifice

Again, it can be easy to slip into some of these situations when you desire to show love or please someone. But having appropriate boundaries protects relationships, places value on both people in the relationship, and produces a healthy context for effective communication.

HERE'S WHERE I DRAW THE LINE ©desdemona72/shutterstock.com

Image Description: An illustration of a person carrying a very large pencil with the words "Here's where I draw the line"

It is easy to see that unhealthy boundaries can be detrimental but why should we set boundaries in the first place and what do they accomplish? The website Habits for Wellbeing (2019) does an excellent job of defining what a boundary is, likening it to a fence or property line.

What Are Personal Boundaries?

Personal boundaries can help us determine and define where our responsibility begins and ends. In addition, they do the following:

- "Keep us safe and see who we are and who we are not"
- "Clarify your needs in a relationship"

- "Provide a moral compass"
- "Are held in place by decisions and actions"

You see, healthy boundaries are action-oriented items—they evolve and change depending on how relationships change; however, there is always the consistent component of mutual respect. We have to be willing to state our boundaries and then honor those boundaries by our behavior.

Finally, let's see what healthy boundaries may look like. How do we go about setting them in our everyday lives? Hereford (2019) says to begin by being clear with YOURSELF that you deserve to have boundaries. You have the right and the personal responsibility to keep yourself safe and healthy. Clarifying what "safe and healthy" means to you is important. There are different aspects of safety—physical, emotional, financial, etc. Take some time to think about these different domains and what it takes in each category to help you feel safe and satisfied. For example, when considering physical safety, you may say that you are not comfortable with people hugging you without asking you first. Emotional safety may involve how others speak to you—the tone of voice that they use, the body language that is employed. Financial safety may involve you needing to keep a minimum amount of money in your savings account to be secure. Whatever the boundary—you have the right and responsibility to communicate that to others.

©Constantin Stanciu/shutterstock.com

Image Description: A photo of a person's hand writing the words "Set boundaries" in a journal

Healthy boundaries are:

- Clear and accurately communicate your needs and wishes—let others know when they have crossed the line in an assertive manner.
- They are articulated early in most relationships so that trust can be built
- They seek to clarify, not confuse.
- They provide a framework from which you interact with others
- They provide others a clear set of expectations—what they can expect from you and how you will treat them as well.
- They are strong. Certainly, boundaries can be adjusted as relationships deepen but a healthy boundary is one that you keep consistently.

ACTIVITY: SETTING BOUNDARIES WORKSHEET
(TherapistAid.com, 2019)

Situation: You invited a friend over for the evening, but now it's getting late. You would like to get ready for bed, but your friend seems unaware of how late it is.

*Response:*_____

Situation: A good friend asks you out on a date. You are not interested in being more than friends. You would like to let them down clearly, but gently.

*Response:*_____

Situation: Your brother asks you to borrow your car. You really don't need it that day but you are worried because he doesn't have a good driving record and you are concerned he will wreck your car.

Reponse: _____

Situation: You have just gotten in from a date with someone who has bought your dinner and movie tickets. They now want to have sex but you are not really ready.

*Response:*_____

Situation: Your take your child to your aunt and uncle's for the holiday. Your aunt tries to give your child a kiss but your child shies away. Your aunt becomes upset.

Response: _____

End of Chapter Self-Reflection

It's time to reflect on what you have learned about yourself through this chapter. Respond to each open-ended prompt on the staircase and save your answers for the culminating planning session at the end of the course.

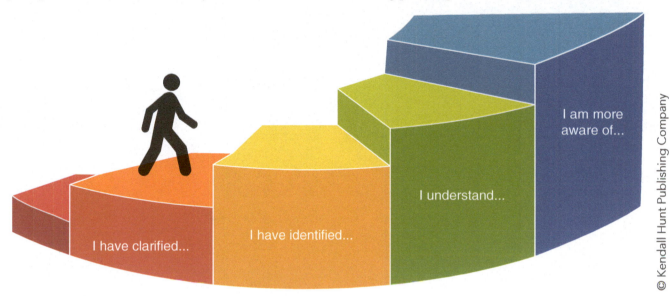

I have clarified...

I have identified...

I understand...

I am more aware of...

© Kendall Hunt Publishing Company

References

4 types of communication styles. (2018). Retrieved from: https://online.alvernia.edu

Habits for Wellbeing. (2019). 15 signs of unhealthy boundaries. Retrieved from https://www.habitsforwellbeing.com/15-signs-of-unhealthy-boundaries/

Hereford, Z. (2019). Healthy personal boundaries and how to establish them. Essential Life Skills. Retrieved from https://www.essentiallifeskills.net/personalboundaries.html

Impact Factory. (2019). Retrieved from https://www.impactfactory.com/library/assertive-communication-6-tips-effective-use

McKay, M., Fanning, D. & Paleg, K. (2006). *Couple Skills: Making Your Relationship Work*. Oakland, CA: New Harbinger Publications, Inc.

TherapistAid.com. (2019). Retrieved from https://www.therapistaid.com/worksheets/setting-boundaries.pdf

UNIT V

Where Am I Going? Career Readiness And Life Mapping

Image Description: A photo of the words "Ready, set, grow"

In this unit, you will take the next steps in your life path—preparing for your career and taking the next step in your "adulting" skills. You will examine myths surrounding career choices and take the next steps to prepare for your job search efforts. Professional communication and preparedness for interviewing will be reviewed. Finally, taking the first steps in creating a solid financial future will be explored.

Image Description: A photo of several light bulbs with the words, "Plan, success, career, skill, goal, development, motivation, and growth inside the bulbs"

©EtiAmmos/shutterstock.com

Chapter Overview

This chapter will highlight some information that will be especially helpful as you transition out of college and start "adulting" full time. Even though we have not focused much on your career specifically throughout this course, all of the information that we covered from personal values and wellness to resiliency and communication, all have implications for success in your future career. The critical skill from this chapter is to discover tools that will enable you to be professional, fiscally responsible, and well-adjusted in your financial life.

In this chapter, you will:

- Explore interesting facts and myths about career
- Learn key points on professionalism in the workplace
- Increase awareness of best financial practices

Critical skill development: By the end of this chapter you should feel prepared to apply and interview for jobs that fit your career plan. Additionally, you should be prepared to take the first steps in creating a solid financial plan that meets your needs and financial goals.

Career Readiness

Image Description: A photo of a goldfish jumping from a small fishbowl into a large fishbowl

One of the realities of life is that sooner or later, we will all have to work. Unless you win the lottery, have really rich relatives, or simply refuse to grow up and just live at home for the rest of your life, eventually you will have to find a job, work, receive a paycheck, and probably pay some bills. While this doesn't sound all that fun, finding a career that fits you, your values, and your personality can be one of the most rewarding things you will ever do. There is a well-known quote by Confucius that says,

"Choose a job you love, and you will never have to work a day in your life."

This may be difficult to believe, but in reality, there are many people who have developed an awareness of what is important to them and then found or developed jobs that were reflections of their dreams. We may have grown up with parents who hated their jobs, grandparents who brought their work home with them, or even had a high school job that made us believe that we would never, ever enjoy working.

But believe it or not, there is some truth to this quote. There is a reason that so many college students agonize over what major to choose; they want to make sure it fits them and that they will not be trapped in a career they hate for the rest of their lives. In addition to that, there are many misconceptions about careers that can intimidate students or make them feel like they are alone in their process.

Top 10 Career Myths

Keep in mind that the road to career happiness is usually full of bumps, curves, and tangents rather than a straight, direct path from point A to point B. The following list will help dispel some common career myths with a good dose of "career reality."

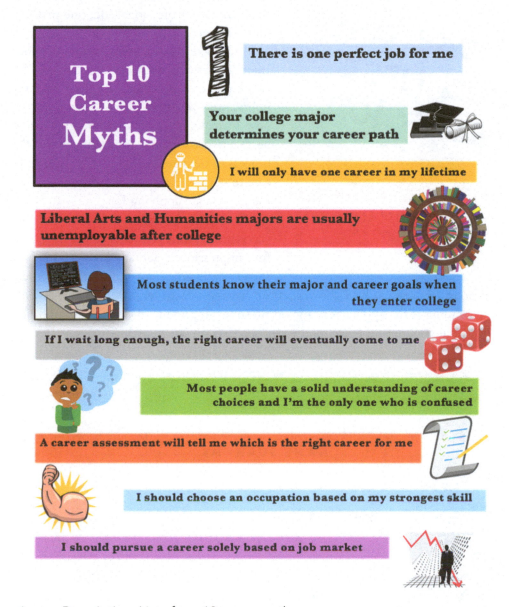

Image Description: List of top 10 career myths.
Source: Bethany Novotny

Image Description: An illustration of a piece of paper with the words "Make a good first impression" written on it

First Impressions

Do you feel confident in making a good first impression? In your professional life, one of the most common situations you will find yourself in where you need to make a good impression is… a job interview! Interviews can be quite intimidating and because they vary based on the organization, job requirements, and interviewer, you may never know what to expect or how to make a strong impression. This section may be able to clarify some common parts of the interview process to prepare for and provide tips so that you are sure to put your best foot forward and hopefully attain the job you are applying for.

First things first, your first impression is not always the first time you meet someone face to face. Your first impression is actually your resume so be sure to spend ample time making it a strong representation of what you have to offer. In fact, studies have shown that on average, a recruiter only spends 6 seconds scanning a resume before determining if the applicant is a good fit, so it's important to catch their attention. Here are some tips for creating your resume and tailoring it to the job that you are applying for.

Image Description: A photo of a resume and a pencil

Tips for creating a resume:

- Be sure that all your contact information is correct and have a professional email address
- Use reverse-chronological order (most recent first)
- Make strategic use of bold, caps, and italics to draw the reader's attention
- Play close attention to formatting and layout and use a standard font
- Consider adding coursework descriptions if you lack job experience
- Include a concise resume summary at the beginning of the document
- Proofread and allow someone else to proofread your resume
- Do not lie on your resume. Not at all. Not ever.
- Match your cover letter to your resume
- Clean up your online presence

Tips for targeting your resume and cover letter to match the job:

- Read the job description carefully... then read it again
- Write a custom resume and cover letter for each job you apply for
- Find and highlight keywords in the duties and skills sections in the job posting
- Include the same keywords that appear in the job description
- Make your job titles as similar as possible to the one in the job ad
- Follow all application instructions provided by the employer

Next, you may score a phone interview. Don't slack off just because this seems a little less formal. Phone interviews can be quite tricky so you need to be prepared and practice. You will not be able to read the interviewers body language so you need to be sure that you are impressive with not only your answers but also how you articulate them. Here are some tips for a successful phone interview:

- Take it as seriously as an in person interview
- Take the call in a comfortable space with limited distractions
- Do some research before the interview
- Listen and don't dominate the conversation
- Slow down and take your time
- Send a thank you email

Finally, the moment you have been waiting for, the face-to-face interview. If you have made it this far in the process, you should be proud. Most employers are sorting through stacks of applicants and only those who are extremely promising are invited to interview. When you secure a face-to-face interview, view it as a wonderful growth opportunity, whether you get offered the job or not. Interviews can be a great way to practice articulating our strengths and communicating how our **transferable skills** can be applied in different settings. Here are some tips for a successful interview:

- Dress for the job (include the organization's primary color in your outfit, if possible)
- Shake hands firmly at the beginning and end of the interview
- Be prepared to answer the following standard questions,
  - "Tell me a little about yourself."
    - By asking this question, interviewers are trying to break the ice and are starting to get a feel for your

Image Description: A photo of two people shaking hands while another person watches

personality. Have your answer to this question rehearsed, otherwise you may end up getting off track and being too long winded. This question is not meant to elicit a long drawn out response about your entire life. Instead, have a standard answer prepared that includes a brief summary of your work and educational background and possibly something personal like a hobby.

- ❑ "What are some of your strengths?"
    - ■ This is another standard interview question that you should be prepared for and have a rehearsed response. Provide 2 to 3 of your best strengths. It would be in your best interest to provide a brief explanation of each and if possible, make a connection between the strength and the job requirements.
- ❑ "What are some of your weaknesses?"
    - ■ This question often leaves people feeling vulnerable and if not practiced ahead of time, can ruin your chances of getting the job. Choose only ONE weakness and follow it up with something positive. For example, "One of my weaknesses is taking on too much. One of the good things about this however is that I manage my time efficiently and I am always able to get everything completed."
- ■ Always be prepared to ask at least one question to the interviewer such as, "when can I expect to hear about the results of the interviews?"
- ■ Send a thank you note or email within 48 hours after the interview
- ■ Clean up your online presence
- ■ Practice, practice, practice!

Now you are ready for the interview, but there is one last concept to revisit—your values. In Chapter 1, you completed the values identification exercise, which laid the groundwork for the entire course. Now that we are near the end of the course, it is important to revisit your values and understand how to apply them and uphold them once you start your career and life outside of college. To do so, let's consider the concept of integrity.

Integrity

Image Description: A photo of a compass pointing to the word "Integrity"

Integrity is defined as consistency of actions, values, methods, measures, principles, expectations, and outcomes. It is regarded as the honesty and truthfulness or accuracy of one's actions. A synonym for integrity is morality. Integrity, simply stated, is behaving in a consistently principled manner no matter who is watching. Integrity is one of the fundamental values that employers seek in the employees that they hire. Here is an example of a dilemma where values and integrity can come into play:

You work as a computer technician for a large casino in Pennsylvania. One of the employee benefits is that you are provided a free meal on your shift but one of the policies is that you are not allowed to take any food home. You realize that there is a lot left over at the end of each day. You have been struggling to keep up with all your bills because you have some significant debt and your mother just had some medical problems that caused you to miss work. You believe it would be really helpful to take some food home so that you can save on groceries for a while but honesty is one of your most esteemed values. Taking some food home would likely not hurt anything but it is against company policy and it would be dishonest. What are your options in this situation and are they integritous?

1.

2.

3.

Research on leadership indicates that integrity is consistently rated as one of the most important character traits of a respected leader. Making sound decisions that are aligned with your personal morals and values is crucial for personal credibility and success in the workplace. Take a moment for some self-reflection and consider the following questions:

a. I always try to do what is right, even when it's costly or difficult. T/ F
b. I am true to my very best self. T/ F
c. I live up to the highest ethical standards. T/ F
d. I don't compromise my values by giving in to temptation. T/ F
e. Your integrity is your gift to yourself and to the world. T/ F
f. I think I am/am not a person of integrity because:
g. Who do you know that you would describe as a person of integrity? What sets this person apart from other people of a similar age and position?
h. Among individuals or groups of people who affect your life directly or indirectly, who has the most integrity? The least?

 Scan the QR code to take the full integrity self-assessment exercise OR follow this link: https://chapters.theiia.org/puget-sound/Documents/Session%201_Integrity-Self-Assessment%20-%20March%202017%20Seattle%20IIA%20Conference.pdf (Integrity Self-Assessment, n.d.).

Professionalism

The email above is an example of many that are received by professors! While the email does get the point across, it is not necessarily the image that you, a young professional, may want to project.

©Titov Nikolai/shutterstock.com

Image Description: An illustration of an envelope with a piece of paper sticking out with the symbol @ written on it

"Hey, do you know when our third quiz is due? I am also going to be late for class tomorrow. My friend's brother is graduating and they want me to be there. So will I miss anything important?"

In previous chapters we have talked a great deal about effective communication—how that communication can build and maintain healthy relationships and how it can ensure that our needs and the needs of others are met. In short, being able to communicate effectively is an invaluable life skill and it permeates every aspect of our lives. The way that we communicate with others says a great deal about who we are and what we believe. Effective communication can convey respect and critical thinking while less effective forms of communication might demonstrate a lack of respect or courtesy. Why have we spent so much time on communication? It is one of the single most important skills that you can master in order to achieve success and yet, we are not typically taught the finer art of communication, particularly when it comes to professional communication.

There are definitely times when communication can be casual—talking to your family or friends is but one example; however, in professional environments, it is often necessary to take your communication skills to the next level. By doing so, you increase the chances of clarity and collaboration—two very important terms in the professional world!

Communication is happening around us at all times and not just verbally. Non-verbal communication is actually the bulk of it! It is not just what you say but how you say it. In addition, aside from traditional ways of communicating (face-to-face), there are an ever-growing number of methods of communication via technology. Most of us are adept users of social media and spend a good number of hours immersed in it. Whether you believe that our increased use of technology is healthy or not, it is certainly here to stay! The purpose of this section is not to argue the validity or benefits of technological communication, even though it is an interesting topic to debate. However, if we are to continue to communicate through technology, it will serve us to better understand how to do effectively and professionally!

©solomon7/shutterstock.com

Image Description: An illustration of various social media site symbols and icons

So let's begin our professional communication journey with one of the most used forms of communication today—the email. Again, the way that you choose to communicate with a close friend or family member may differ dramatically but in general, it works out well when basic rules of email etiquette are used.

Email

When drafting an email, please keep **"tone"** in mind first and foremost. You want the recipient to not only get your message loud and clear but you want for them to feel as if they have been communicated with in a professional tone. While it is common practice to use emojis in text messages (more on that later!) it is less common to use them in emails and for professional communications, emojis are not appropriate. Therefore, without a smiling little head in the email, you must be careful that the words that you choose are respectful and friendly. It can help to read your completed email out loud to "listen for tone." Ambiguous language or a choppy syntax might convey a lack of respect or warmth. If you read over the email and find the tone to be problematic, go back and revise your email until you are satisfied that the tone is appropriate.

Now that we have considered tone, we can follow a "recipe" for constructing a professional email. Let's look at an example of an email that works.

Dear Professor Sherman,

I hope that you are having a nice day today. My name is Bryson Baker and I am a student in your Wednesday afternoon Child Psychology class. As I was leaving class this afternoon, I realized that I had an unanswered question. I have reviewed the syllabus and course materials but have been unable to find the answer. Are we required to write our final exam paper in APA or MLA style? Thank you so much for offering clarification.
Sincerely,
Bryson Baker
bakerb@etsu.edu
Cell: 123-555-5487

What Makes This Email Effective? Let's Take A Closer Look

Begins with professional title

Quickly tells who is sending the email and from what class

udes nice eting

Dear Professor Sherman,

I hope that you are having a nice day today. My name is Bryson Baker and I am a student in your Wednesday afternoon Child Psychology class. As I was leaving class this afternoon, I realized that I had an unanswered question. I have reviewed the syllabus and course materials but have been unable to find the answer. Are we required to write our final exam paper in APA or MLA style? Thank you so much for offering clarification.

Demonstrates that you have tried to answer the question on your own

Clearly states question

Sincerely,   Gratitude

Bryson Baker   Full name and contact info
bakerb@etsu.edu
Cell: 123-555-5487

Although the email is not lengthy, it does a good job of conveying warmth and responsibility. You have given the recipient everything that they need to respond and have done so in a respectful manner. **Every email should be proof-read for clarity, grammar, and misspellings.**

Now using the template provided, construct your own email to one of your professors, asking a question.

Dear _____,

_____

_____

_____

_____

_____

Texting

In general, we usually think of texts as a more informal type of communication. It is often used with friends and family; however, there is the occasion when you may have to use text messaging with a supervisor or colleague. In that case, following the basic email etiquette rules will be helpful.

- Always identify yourself in the text with a full name. The person that you are texting may not recognize your number.
- Keep texts brief. If you must convey a great deal of information, it is likely best to either call the recipient or send an email.
- Avoid using emojis or other shorthand such as LOL, BTW, etc. Type words out fully to avoid any miscommunications.
- Provide an alternate way to reach you in response such as an email address in case the recipient prefers another mode of communication.

When sending texts, always make sure that auto correct hasn't left you a surprise!

In any written communication, such as letters, emails, or texts, it is helpful to review what you have written thoroughly before sending it. Remember, your correspondence often serves as your first impression and you want for it to be a strong, professional impression!

Phone and Voice Mail

As texts have grown in popularity, phone calls seem to have decreased; however, they do still happen! When you are making or taking a professional call, please pay attention to the following guidelines suggested by Ransom Patterson in their Beginner's Guide to Professional Communication (Patterson, 2017).

- **Listen more than you talk.** This is good advice for any kind of personal interaction.
- **Pause.** This goes along with listening. When you're speaking to someone in person, you have visual cues that help you tell if they're about to say something. On the phone, you just have a lower quality version of their voice. When someone is answering a question or telling you something, pause for a moment afterward. That gives them a chance to add anything additional without you interrupting them.
- **Avoid long silences.** On the other hand, don't let long silences hang. The other person may think you've hung up or aren't paying attention. It's a balancing act.
- **Don't be afraid to ask for clarification.** On the phone, details of speech can be lost. If you didn't understand numbers or a name or anything else that person said, ask them politely to repeat it or spell it. It's better to ask once than to end up with the wrong information—that just slows everyone down.

- **Identify yourself and then ask to whom you're speaking.** It's general phone etiquette. Begin every business phone call with, *Hello, this is [YOUR FULL NAME] from [YOUR ORGANIZATION AND/ OR TITLE]. Is this [PERSON'S NAME AND TITLE]?* If you don't know who the other person is, you can ask *To whom am I speaking?* Besides being polite, it gets the call off to an efficient start and avoids an awkward pause at the beginning.

- **Take notes.** Take notes on the important details of the call. That way, you have info in case you need to follow up with the person via email or other means.

- **Leaving a voicemail.** Always identify yourself with your FULL name and your association with the person that you are calling. Leave a *brief* message that quickly and succinctly covers the reason for your call and leave a full number or other contact information where you can be reached for follow up.

Social Media

We love our social media sites! And why not? They can be informative, educational, entertaining, and most of all, fun! With the myriad of sites available today, we can find our niche somewhere and become immersed. These sites should be fun and personal, but the simple fact is that they are *not* personal—what we put out on social media is there for all to see in many instances and it lives forever on the internet. While it would be nice to be able to fully limit who sees what—it is simply not guaranteed and therefore, if we wish to be viewed as professional, we must be cognizant of what we share and post on social media sites.

Consider this…should you post anything that you think a potential supervisor or better yet, your mother, wouldn't approve of? Ha! While we're just joking here, there might be some truth to the question! Ultimately the decision of what to post and share is yours but if you decide that you want to err on the safe side, the following guidelines might be helpful (Satterfield, 2016).

Financial Competence: A Big Step in Planning Your Future

As a student, graduating from high school and jumping through all the hoops for college, application, financial aid applications, SATs/ACTs, and scholarship applications, has most likely consumed your thoughts. And now you are here…a poor college student! Most college students experience financial difficulties and insecurity during their college years. The trick is to confine those difficulties and insecurities JUST to college years and not beyond.

To do that requires discipline and planning at a time in life that newfound freedoms are also happening. College students are tasked with significant life transitions and adjustments overnight. One moment you are

Image Description: Photo of a piggy bank and a chalk board that says "financial planning."

©kenary820/shutterstock.com

a high school senior with rules and curfews and allowances and restrictions. Then POOF! You have graduated, are a college student, and considered to be an adult. Financial lending institutions are very interested in your newfound freedom and the need for funding for college. They market to that need and offer deals that sound too good to be true…because they are! College students are bombarded with offers for student loans and other lending opportunities. AND THE KEY TERMS HERE ARE: LOAN AND LENDING! As in those monies have to be paid back. The terms of these loans and other lending opportunities can be confusing, so do not sign until you completely understand what you are agreeing to pay back. As a legal adult, this debt and responsibility is on your shoulders now.

Image Description: Stacks of coins with plants growing out of the top.

One of the keys to having a successful post college adult life is to have financial freedom. That was the actual purpose of attending college, right? To obtain an education to get a degree that leads to a career that is fulfilling and provides financially for your life needs and wants. Unfortunately, the trend is that students are leaving college with massive student loan debt that financially ties their hands from living their best adult life. Right here, right now, you have the opportunity to NOT do that to yourself and get off to a better start in your post college adult life. While you may feel that you have no control, you actually do. You have control because you have choices in how you live your college life.

A college advisor shared two student stories: Caitlin and Michael.

Caitlin came in to see her advisor and was very stressed. The source of her stress was that she was not making the grades that she needed in her courses. She related that the source of her struggle was her excessive work hours that kept her from completing the course work and also impacted her attendance. When asked, Caitlin stated she worked at least 30 hours each week and sometimes 40 hours per week. She had signed student loans as well and at the end of her sophomore year, she would have accrued $15,000 in student loan debt. She had at least 2 more years to complete her degree and her anticipated loan debt at that time was going to be $32,000. The mounting debt was severely adding to Caitlin's stress.

Image Description: The word "debt" being pushed over a cliff.

To begin to help her, the advisor asked about her living arrangements and bills so that they could look at some options to reduce expenses to reduce the amount of work hours and loans for Caitlin. Caitlin had chosen to live with 2 of her friends in a new apartment complex designed for students that offered a coffee bar, swimming pool, and gym as part of the amenities. She had incurred shopping debt on high interest rate credit cards. Caitlin was proud of her appearance and had weekly manicures as well as monthly salon visits to color and style her hair. When she came to college, she had asked for her own cell phone plan separate from her family's plan so that she could have unlimited usage and other features. All of these "amenities" had added up to an extravagant amount of money for a college student to earn. To cover the gap, Caitlin had taken out the max amount in student loans.

The advisor talked with Caitlin about choices she had made that led her to this place of financial difficulty and what she was willing to choose (or choose to live without) in order to reduce her debt and to be more successful in her college career. Caitlin was taken aback at first, but then began to consider healthier options for her financial life so that her adult life might be better.

The next day, the advisor met with Michael. Michael was doing well in his classes. He had two semesters left to finish his degree and he very proudly said he had managed to do so with no debt. He was a first generation college student and said his parents did not have much money to help him with college so he had been working his way through. He said, "It hasn't always been pretty, but I have made it work." Michael's plan had been to make choices that paid him to go to school and not the other way around. He applied for absolutely every scholarship, no matter how small, that came his way. He stated he hated writing the essays for them, but figured the hour it took for him to potentially earn $500 scholarship was a good paycheck and there was no job he could get that would pay him $500 and hour. So, he buckled down and wrote the essays. He lived in an apartment that he described as "nothing fancy, but safe" with four other guys which made his living expenses minimal. He worked for the food service agency on the college campus so his meals were free as part of his job, further reducing his expenses. He said, "I don't eat out much because it is expensive, but I have plenty of food through my job." He could ride his bike to campus, which is also where he worked, and save on gas. He only drove his beater car on weekends. Michael cut corners everywhere he could and as a college senior—had zero debt. The advisor was very impressed with Michael. She asked Michael what encouraged him to make these choices. Michael said, "I am here to get a future so that I can live a better life and have a better lifestyle. I knew I couldn't have all the "things" that I might want now, but

Image Description: Sunset image with a dollar sign and a person flexing.

being smart about my money would pay off later. It really hasn't been easy, but now that I am near the finish line, those choices have paid off for me and seem worth it."

The difference between Caitlin and Michael was their focus on long-term goals and discipline in the moment to take them one step forward to reaching those goals. Financial competence at this stage of a college student's life is critical to a more financially successful future.

One further step that Michael had taken was to consult with a financial planner. Michael stated, "I have ended a paycheck period with $50 extra dollars and I really wanted to just go out and spend it, but I knew the next month I might be $50 short, so I started saving it. After a little while I had some money, $300, put away, and I was tempted to spend it. SO, I found a financial planner that would work with students and started my plan. That $300 is now safely put away and drawing interest. It is there if I need it, it is still my money and I can access it if I need it, but it is safe from my temptation to spend it, because I really, really wanted the new cell phone that came out."

For students who have little to no extra funds to spare, a financial plan is still very important for managing debt, repayment of that debt, and future planning. Having a plan brings a sense of control and peace about a

Image Description: A hand pointing to a cyclical process about financial planning.

financial future. There are online resources, books, courses, and a large selection of financial planning institutions to support this process. The key is to find the one that is right for you. Doing your research and interviewing several financial planners and financial planning institutions is the smartest way to start your selection process.

Long-term financial planning goals are important. Financial planner, Dustin Jackson (2019) shared the following as the most successful and practical financial advice for anyone; regardless of their age:

1. Have an emergency fund—this is money that you have set aside either in a savings, checking, or money market fund. This money is very liquid and accessible at any time. The general rule of thumb is to have between 3 and 6 months of your basic living expenses in your emergency fund. This money can be available to you if unexpected expenses come up, which always do. It is also nice to have an emergency fund if you find yourself between jobs, this allows you to continue to pay for all necessary expenses and not have to add debt to your financial picture.

2. Payoff or reduce debt—This is the next step after you have established your emergency fund. I first like to organize all debts from the smallest to largest (in dollar amounts) and then find the amount of interest you are paying on each of those debts. So how do we go about paying down these debts?

   - One way is to start paying off the debt that has the highest interest rate first and then systematically paying all debts off from the highest to the lowest interest rate.
   - Another way is to simply take your smallest debt (in dollar amounts) & pay it off first, then tackling the larger debts last. This can sometimes help with not getting discouraged in the payoff process since you will have some victories along the way.
   - The bottom line is being smart with debt. Try not to go into debt if it all possible, but if you already find yourself in debt, hopefully, the above ideas can help you at least get an established plan to reverse your way out of debt so you will be able to pay yourself not the bank.

3. Now that you have an emergency fund and your debt is paid off. You can now start investing for your future. There are many different options that can help you prepare for retirement. Some of the most popular ways to save for retirement are:

   - Your employer sponsored retirement plan. 401(k)
   - An individual retirement account "IRA"
     - Traditional IRA—before tax savings/taxable when you withdraw
     - Roth IRA—after tax savings/ so tax-free withdrawals in retirement
   - Brokerage/investment account
   - Real estate

4. Protection

   - Auto insurance—make sure you have appropriate amount of coverage. Ex: 500k/300k/500k
   - Homeowners/renters insurance—protect against loss of home or contents you have while in rental property.
   - Health insurance—this is a must. It only takes one major health event to derail the greatest investment strategy. If your employer does not offer health insurance in their benefits package, then I highly recommend getting an individual health policy.
   - General liability insurance—once you have accumulated assets, it's common you may want to protect them in the event of a lawsuit. This type of insurance is also referred to as an umbrella policy.
   - Life insurance—protect the ones you love the most from the unexpected. Who depends on the income you

Image Description: A piggy bank air balloon.

©Lightspring/shutterstock.com

©iQoncept/shutterstock.com

Image Description: A paved road with the words "debt free!"

generate from your job? What debts would you like to be paid off in the event of your passing? Would you like to make sure your spouse and kids are taken care of and their retirement and education plans remain on solid footing?

- Disability insurance—protect your income stream in the event you become disabled and can no longer work. There are two types of disability coverage; short and long term. I recommend that you have both. Most employers offer both of these within their total benefits package, usually at a reasonable price. You can purchase an individual policy if not offered through your employer, but you may expect to pay a little more in premium. Most major insurance companies offer this type of coverage.

End of Chapter Self-Reflection

It's time to reflect on what you have learned about yourself through this chapter. Respond to each open-ended prompt on the staircase and save your answers for the culminating planning session at the end of the course.

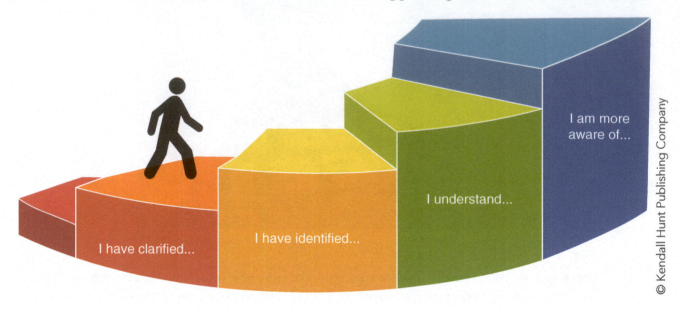

I am more aware of...

I understand...

I have identified...

I have clarified...

© Kendall Hunt Publishing Company

References

Integrity Self-Assessment. (n.d.). Retrieved from https://chapters.theiia.org/puget-sound/Documents/Session%201_Integrity-Self-Assessment%20-%20March%202017%20Seattle%20IIA%20Conference.pdf

Jackson, D. (2019). Interview and notes provided for financial planning success.

Patterson, R. (2017). The beginner's guide to professional communication. Retrieved from https://collegeinfogeek.com/professional-communication-guide/

Satterfield, H. (2016). Social media do's and don'ts for college students. Retrieved from https://sysomos.com/2016/11/10/social-media-dos-donts-college-students/

CHAPTER 9
Life Mapping: The Plan

Putting It All Together

Image Description: A photo of a person framing the sun with their fingers

In the busyness of daily living, sometimes our life plan is forgotten or pushed to the side. All the wonderful ideas and directions you have for your life swim out of focus. This exercise is to help you retain that focus and intentionality in your life so that you get where you want to go and become the person you want to be. It is important to have direction and the development of your life plan is intended to help you keep that focus. ***NOTE TO USING THIS GUIDE:*** The best use of this tool is to make it a living, breathing document. It grows and changes as you grow and change. Keeping it handy so that you can refer back to it regularly is important. Equally important is retooling and recalibrating. If a goal or action becomes irrelevant to you or needs adjusting, DO IT! Do not feel obligated to work toward a goal that is no longer fitting if your life course and focus needs a shift. Rewrite it! The important idea here is that this is a living guide to YOU! Make it work for YOU ~ **YOU ARE THE AUTHOR OF YOUR OWN STORY!**

This last chapter is a working chapter that pulls together all the thoughts, ideas, and self-discoveries that have occurred throughout this course. You will be referring back to work you completed, but as you are filling in these blanks—you should make any changes and updates that you want.

Value Statements: The Big Three [From Chapter One]

Restate your top three value statements. Your value statements should provide the foundation for the direction of your life. Keeping them in focus keeps you on track! Room is provided for three, but you include as many of your values as you like—whatever has meaning to you.

Image Description: Cogs of a wheel with the words "Core Values" dominantly displayed

Value One: I want to live my life in a way that

Value Two: I want to live my life in a way that

Value Three: I want to live my life in a way that

The Key Questions

These key questions were the guiding questions to the work you have done in this course. Take a moment to collect your thoughts based on the work you have done. Review the answers you posted to these questions in the chapters as indicated and copy your answer to the key questions below. You may want to take this opportunity to add or update your thoughts as you transfer this information over. Space is also provided for you to add key questions to these if you so wish.

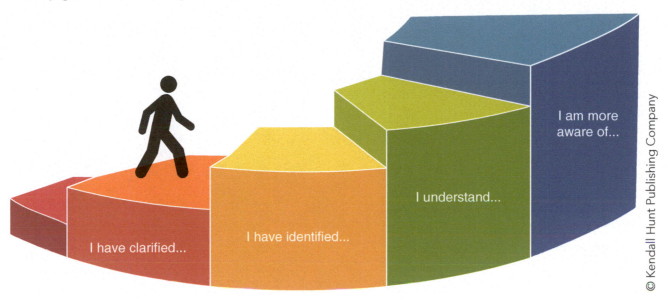

UNIT I: Who Am I? (Chapters 1 and 2)

I have clarified . . .

I have identified . . .

I understand . . .

I am more aware of . . .

UNIT II: Why Am I Here? (Chapters 3 and 4)

I have clarified . . .

I have identified . . .

I understand . . .

I am more aware of . . .

UNIT III: Personal Resources, Assets, and Aptitudes (Chapters 5 and 6)

I have clarified . . .

I have identified . . .

I understand . . .

I am more aware of . . .

UNIT IV: Relationships and Connections (Chapter 7)

I have clarified . . .

I have identified . . .

I understand . . .

I am more aware of . . .

UNIT V: Where Am I Going? (Chapters 8 and 9)

I have clarified . . .

I have identified . . .

I understand . . .

I am more aware of . . .

©13_Phunkod/shutterstock.com

Image Description: An illustration of a person standing inside a light bulb with their arms outstretched with sparkling lights surrounding them

And finally, add your **Light Bulb Moments**. These are the insights and realizations that came to you as you worked through this text. Maybe one of the thought bubbles gave you an inspiration, maybe a class colleague offered an insight that was significant, maybe one of the quotes, internet time-outs or reading passages gave you pause—whatever that may be—jot down your ideas and keynotes here:

Image Description: An illustration of a highway leading into the distance with the words "Are you ready?" written on the road

From all of the information above—begin to craft your Life Plan. Blank pages can be intimidating, so start with a creative doodle like we have practiced before. You get to be creative here or very structured here— YOUR PLAN—YOUR WAY. This is YOU making a plan for YOUR LIFE. You determine:

- The way it looks
- The time intervals you are planning (1 week, 1 month, 1 year, 5 years, or more)
- The personal and professional growth that occurs at each GIANT STEP
- Any other details you want to include

Suggestions are:

- Make it visually appealing to you
- Make it simple and clean—if you want to include more details, put it on the back of the guide
- Note time frames for reviewing the guide and your progress so adjustments can be made

Image Description: A person making a long leap from one rock to another over water with the sun shining and blue skies over them

Take a moment, a few deep breaths, and GO!